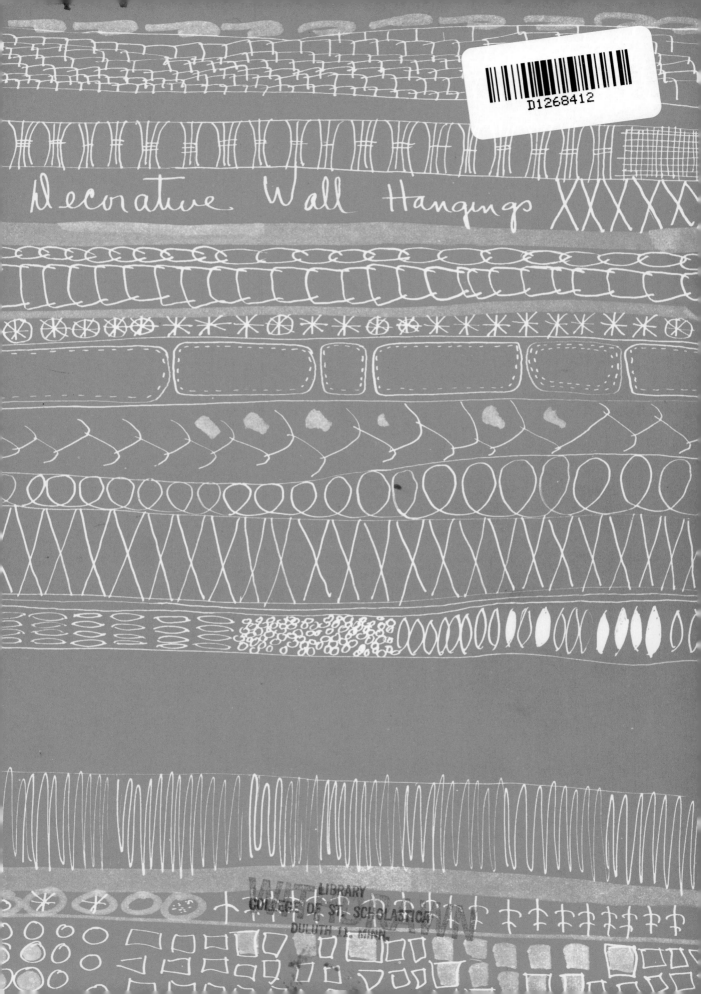

Decorative Wall Hangings

decorative wall hangings

decorative
wall hangings

art with fabric

by david b. van dommelen

funk & wagnalls company, inc.

To my wife, who understands my creative ambitions and
helps me with enthusiastic encouragement.

preface

This book on decorative wall hangings has been prepared in the hope that it will act as a resource and guide manual for the crafts- man, the educator, and the homemaker. There are few books concerning this medium on the market today, in view of the many artists who are creatively involved in the production of wall hangings. Much of the work being exhibited is of experimental nature and is good, but much is being produced that lacks direction, craftsman- ship, and understanding of the medium by the artist.

It is for these reasons that I have attempted to collect and organize this book for those beginners who wish to get a start in an exciting and inspiring craft. For those who have already taken the first steps, it will provide an introduction to many outstanding artists con- tributing to the world of crafts and arts for the home: their goals and philosophies, their methods and materials, and their place in 20th- century contemporary design.

I do not pretend to provide complete answers for either group, but rather a brief look into a creative and artistic expression that is rapidly taking its place next to the fine arts.

D.B.V.D.

acknowledgments

The completion of this book would not have been possible without the efforts of many people. These generous people I would like to thank for their interest and courtesy in helping me with some of the problems with the manuscript. I wish to thank especially Sam Richardson, Director of Research at the American Craftsmen's Council, and his staff for their kind assistance in providing photographs; the many craftsmen who have sent and given me permission to use photographs of their work; Pennsylvania State University for financial help in obtaining some of the photographs for this work; and special thanks to Jean Ray Laury, who read parts of my manuscript and gave me added encouragement through her letters to me.

ix

contents

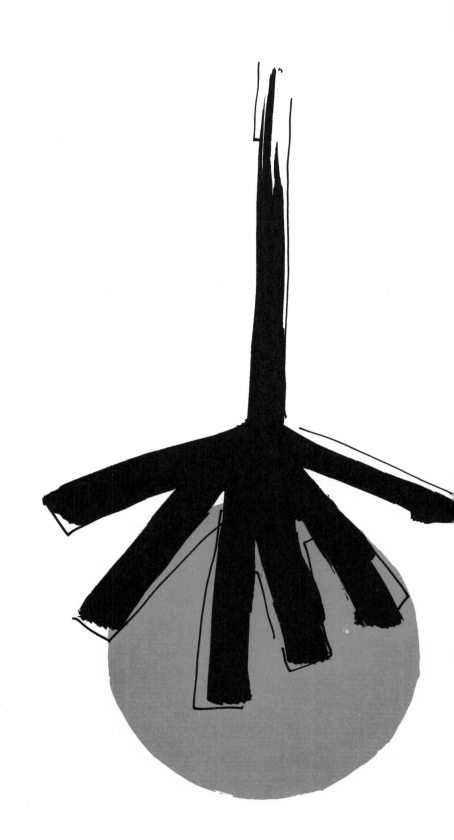

Embroidery is a challenge to your imagination and makes it possible for you
to express ideas with a needle. Any person who can sew a fine seam should,
within a short time, develop into a painter in thread.

mariska karasz

Adventures in Stitches

decorative wall hangings

1. Petroglyphs, Burro Flats, California
Petroglyphs in caves are good examples of the manner in which primitive man surrounded himself with beauty. The petroglyphs pictured here are painted in black, white, red, orange, and pink.

historical background

Throughout the history of mankind, man has been interested in, and has surrounded himself with, beautiful objects and places in which to live, and he has endeavored to ornament the walls of his home beyond utilitarian needs. Many of these wall decorations are the result of religious experiences; some can be associated with the preservation of tribal customs; others are merely designs that satisfy the need for enrichment to delight the eye.

The purpose of this book is not to present a detailed and complex study of the history of wall decorations, but it seems appropriate at this time to point out some of the achievements in this creative field which has flourished for so many centuries on our earth.

From the multitude of textile accomplishments in the past, only a few are directly related to wall-hanging design. However, many of the textile arts that were practiced by primitive man and in cultures around the world have contributed techniques that are the basis for all contemporary expression by today's artist-craftsman. The textile designer has built his working vocabulary liberally on this rich heritage, and would be dishonest if he rejected what past generations have left him. It is possible to look at only a few isolated examples of this library of techniques in textiles, and through these limited samples to hope that the reader will build his knowledge through continued reading, research, and experimental work.

2. Bayeux Tapestry

The Bayeux Tapestry, sometimes referred to as the Tapestry of Queen Matilda, was made about 1180 A.D. of worsted wool embroidered on linen. The tapestry is unique of its kind, for most early medieval works of art have religious rather than secular themes.

Courtesy of the Bayeux Cathedral Museum, Bayeux, France

Although we will generally be concerned with decorative motifs that are attached to the wall after completion, we might mention some of the early cave adornments that were applied directly to some surface. Decorations incised or painted directly on the surface of cave walls and rocks certainly meant more to the primitive man than the decorative wall hangings with which we adorn our homes today mean to us. It is highly unlikely that early cave paintings were created solely for embellishment. Instead, they were probably used as religious symbols, or were connected with various dream visions of a mythological nature. The important element is that primitive man, from the cave dweller of southern France to the American Indian of the Southwest, felt an urgency to leave his creative mark on the walls that surrounded him. Even though his reasons differed from ours, still he was concerned, as we are, with creative achievement.

The petroglyphs of Burro Flats in California (fig. 1) are a good example of how early man decorated his walls. These line drawings created several thousand years ago by Indians of the North American continent were probably painted to insure success in the hunt. Parts of them seem to be only designs, and other parts seem to represent human figures. Through these primitive cave paintings we can see that man has always been concerned with beauty, and, from this first creative exercise, observe how the decorating of walls developed into many varied channels of expression.

Because we are primarily interested in the development of wall hangings, we might look briefly at one that stands out in the history of Western man. The Bayeux Tapestry (fig. 2) is probably the most celebrated piece of embroidery in the Western world. It was completed in the latter part of the 12th century to portray the invasion of England by William the Conqueror. Although it is only 19 inches high, its overall length exceeds 200 feet. Embroidered with beautiful worsteds on linen, it is one of the masterpieces of art from medieval Europe. The unusual thing about the Bayeux Tapestry is that it commemorates and records historical events of the time, rather than a religious story. This is not to say that other wall hangings of this era never portrayed secular happenings, but only to point out that this was an uncommon subject for a wall hanging at this time in history.

Very similar to the work of the Bayeux Tapestry is the work by Icelandic craftsmen on the Holar Altarpiece (fig. 3). During the

3. Holar Tapestry
Example of early Scandinavian stitchery used as an altarpiece.

Hanns Reich Verlag

15th century in Iceland, the long winter months stimulated the weavers to design and execute very elaborate religious tapestries and embroideries for the altars of the churches in which they worshiped. The fishermen who traveled to Europe told on their return of beautiful hangings decorating the churches and castles of the rich, and these accounts had a heavy influence on the work accomplished in Iceland. Although the hangings for the churches were done by accomplished craftsmen, the women of the island also worked industriously on utilitarian objects for the home. Both groups of objects were worked in the finest wool, coming from the beautiful sheep of the Icelandic mountainside. The Holar Altarpiece in the Holar Cathedral of Iceland is probably one of the finest pieces of craftsmanship in Scandinavia. It is very different from the Bayeux Tapestry in subject, but there is an overall likeness in feeling. Both are clearly two-dimensional, and the figures in both seem to be frozen into their positions, as is typical of medieval art. However, the Holar Altarpiece is somewhat more rich in color, and has a completely filled-in background, which of course is possible only because of its much smaller size.

8

4. The Hunt of the Unicorn

A late 15th-century French or Flemish tapestry showing the unicorn being brought to the castle. This tapestry is of wool and silk, with silver and silver-gilt threads.

The Metropolitan Museum of Art, The Cloisters Collection,
Gift of John D. Rockefeller, Jr., 1937

Although the actual techniques of true tapestry weaving will not be presented in this book, it is such an important step in wall decoration that it should not be passed without mention. Tapestry weaving appears to have started no later than the 9th century, but it rose to its height in the 15th and 16th centuries. "In tapestry, the design is woven into the fabric itself by a process of winding the weft or woof, the name given the horizontal threads, around the warp or vertical ones, the work all being executed by hand and the stitches pressed tightly against each other so that the warp is entirely covered by the woof." (Art in the Western World, Robb and Garrison, p.913) The most outstanding examples of tapestry work from this period on view in the United States are the Unicorn tapestries at the Cloisters Museum in New York (fig. 4). Unfortunately, their source has never been determined, but certainly they reflect the creative achievements in the tapestry field. They very closely resemble the Unicorn series which hangs in the Cluny Museum in Paris. The series of seven tapestries in the Cloisters represents secular matter, yet the hangings are filled with religious symbolism and allegory. Two of the most important factories producing tapestries were in France. Gobelin and Aubusson both played a major role in medieval tapestry design. In recent years many French artists have taken an active interest in the design and production of tapestries, and their work has been traveling through the United States in exhibitions.

Decorative wall hangings were not unique to Europe. Asia contributed much to the textile world. Embroidery was at its finest in the days of the Chinese dynasties in the Orient. It was there that crewelwork became so meticulous that it was later outlawed because of the danger of blindness involved in its execution. The minute, delicate stitches were laid closely next to each other, and the pieces of clothing and hangings produced excelled those of any other period in history. The Chinese craftsmen worked in beautiful representational forms that bordered on the abstract. Their work was rich and colorful in subject matter, as we see in the Emperor's Dragon Medallion (fig. 5), created in the Ming Dynasty between the 14th and 17th centuries.

In India, textile design has flourished for two thousand years, and techniques have been developed that highly influenced our English-speaking culture. "Such names as *calico, sash, shawl, pajama,*

The Metropolitan Museum of Art, Anonymous, 1946

5. Emperor's Dragon Medallion
The delicate crewelwork in this Chinese textile was done during the Ming Dynasty (1368-1644).

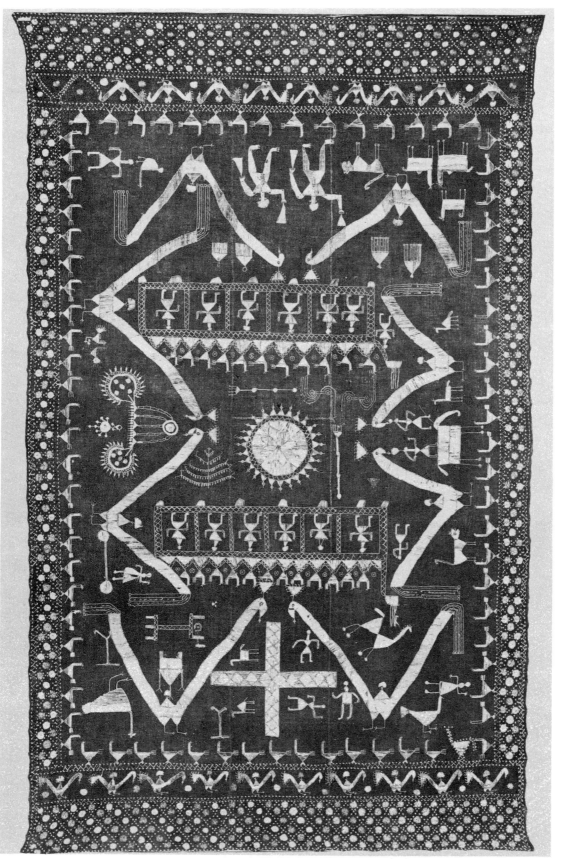

6. Indian Embroidery
A dark-green embroidered cotton hanging illustrates for us some of the interesting stitchery
of Kangra or Chamba in the early 19th century.

7. Rumal Embroidery
An example of stitchery from the late 18th century in India, probably showing everyday
activities in the home.

gingham, dimity . . ." (*Textiles and Ornaments of India*, p. 26) are only a few of the Indian words that we have seen introduced into our textile vocabulary. The textiles of India include weaving, embroidery, tie-dyeing, block printing, and other exciting methods of work. Generally these techniques were applied to clothing textiles, but, as in the curtain from Kangra (fig. 6), they were also used for purely decorative purposes. Linear compositions of scenes of animals and people show us the sophistication of 19th century folk art in India. This piece is typical of the craftsmanship traditionally executed by the native women in the villages. In their work are many stitches with which we are familiar, especially satin stitch, chain stitch, and cross-stitch. Each region of India has styles distinctive in approach to color, design, and technique.

In South America, too, the natives excelled in creative textile design, and from Mexico to Chile many types of approaches in technique were utilized. These textiles were used for clothing, as well as for shrouds in subterranean tombs. The tapestry work of Peru was complex, technically perfect, and rich in color and texture (fig. 8). In some respects it is considered much finer than European tapestry work. Sometimes up to 500 weft threads are incorporated in a one-inch area. But what is unique in the tapestries of the area is that the embroidery is superimposed on the finished weft side; in some instances it is applied to both sides. As we see in the Peruvian tapestry, mythological monsters and creatures—terrifying demons, half human, half animal—were used for subject matter.

Certainly not as old in tradition, but just as exciting as the early Peruvian textiles, are the imaginative *molas* (blouses) of the San Blas Islands, off the coast of Panama (fig. 9). Here the women of this primitive present-day culture decorate their apparel with delicate, meticulous, yet bold appliqué work. The *mola* symbolizes wealth to the San Blas woman, and so she tries to bring her collection of blouses to a goodly number before her marriage. Often the designs are based on objects of modern civilization which find their way to the islands; it is startling to see, for example, a cigarette-package motif incorporated into the pattern. Aside from such whimsical intrusions, the pieces of fabric show objects and events from the daily life of the San Blas Indians. Obviously the *mola* is not meant by the local Indians to be used as a wall hanging, but the technique has fascinated many contemporary artists; tourists return-

14

ing from these islands highly prize pieces of the appliquéd fabric as decorative hangings for their homes. You will see later that some of the work by Jean Ray Laury has the same intricate qualities as the work produced by the San Blas women.

A few highlights of the craftsman's heritage in textiles have been pointed out to the reader. Obviously, only a small portion could be presented in this brief historical introduction, but this is enough to make the beginner aware of the huge number of resources that are available to the interested artist and layman. Stitchery, appliqué, block and screen printing, tapestry, and many other techniques used in clothing, household objects, and decorative textiles in past and primitive societies are being reintroduced, and are fast taking an important role in our contemporary world of crafts. It is interesting to note here that not only professional craftsmen are making wide use of these varied methods; educational institutions have also taken part in the revival of textile arts. In schools across the country, small children are experiencing new forms of expression in threads and fabrics (fig. 10). Teachers have found that they can offer the child of today a technique that is new to him, yet easily manageable, and a craft that can speak to the child at many different levels of skill and sensitivity. Students in university programs of Art Education, Applied Arts, and Home Economics are finding a challenging medium in which to express their philosophies. Having discovered the world of textiles, many of these students continue experimenting and exploring, much as a painter would do in the "fine arts," and thus they join the growing circle of artist-craftsmen.

8. Embroidery, Tiahuanaco II
Detail of an embroidered mantle from the south coast of Peru, near Pisco. This piece dates from before 1000 A.D.

Museum of Fine Arts, Boston

From the Collection of Miss Phoebe Harris

17

9. San Blas Indian Fabric
This meticulously appliquéd fabric comes from the San Blas Indians. The craftsmanship looks much like that of Jean Ray Laury, a contemporary American wall-hanging designer.

10. Cooperative Wall Hanging
Children pooled their creative efforts to realize this fine stitchery.
Courtesy of Cordelia Jennett, Public Schools, Kansas City, Mo.

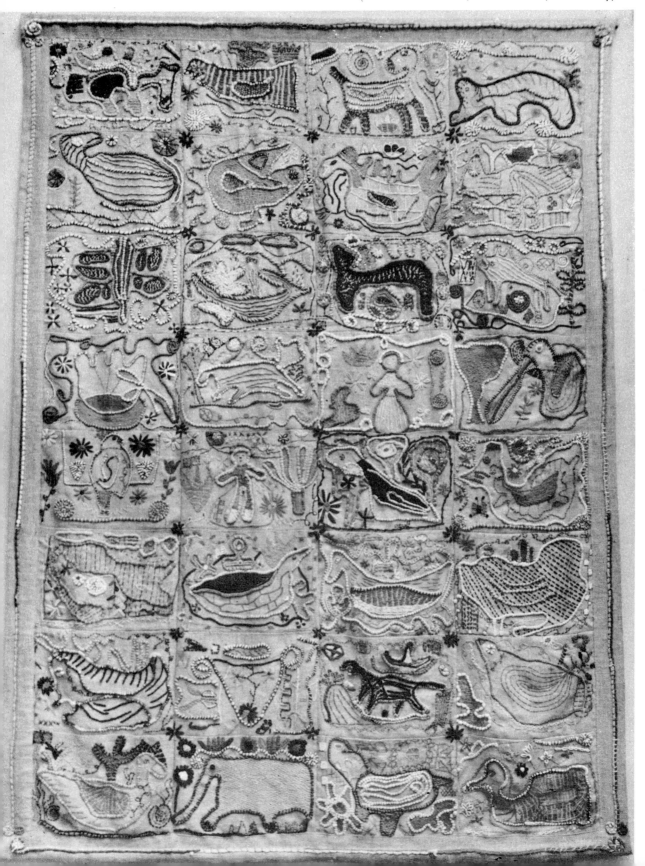

11. Midnight Gardens *by Van Dommelen*
A decorative wall hanging showing the contemporary uses of appliqué and stitchery.

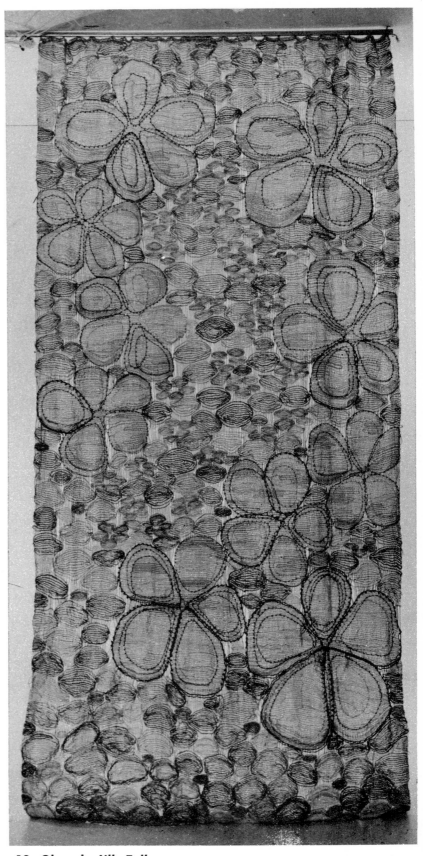

20

12. Olvon *by Ulla Tollerz*
A transparent experiment in gobelin technique uses hand-spun linen yarns dyed in the ancient manner of cooking flowers, leaves, and roots to obtain the colors.

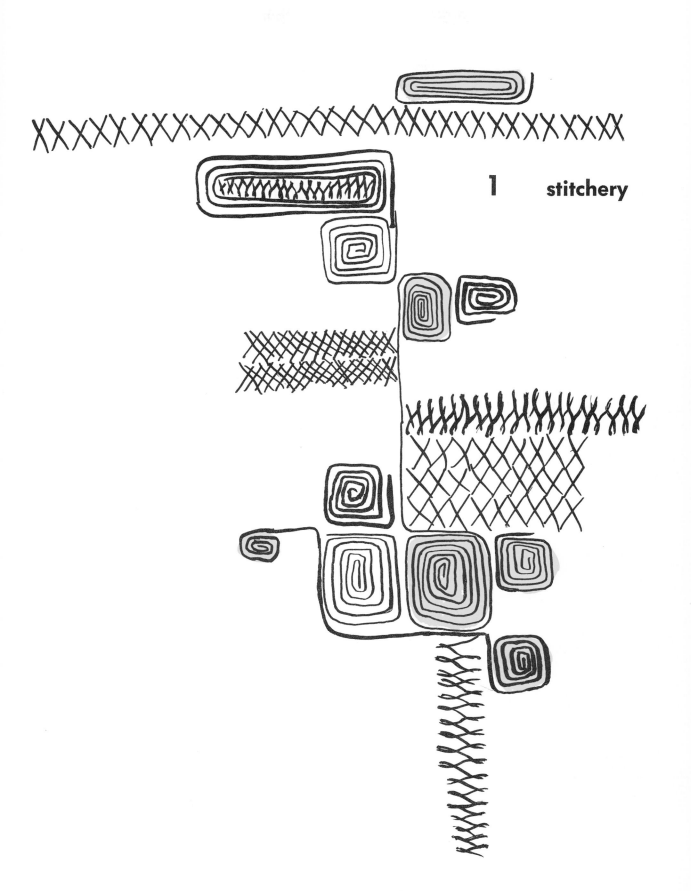

1 stitchery

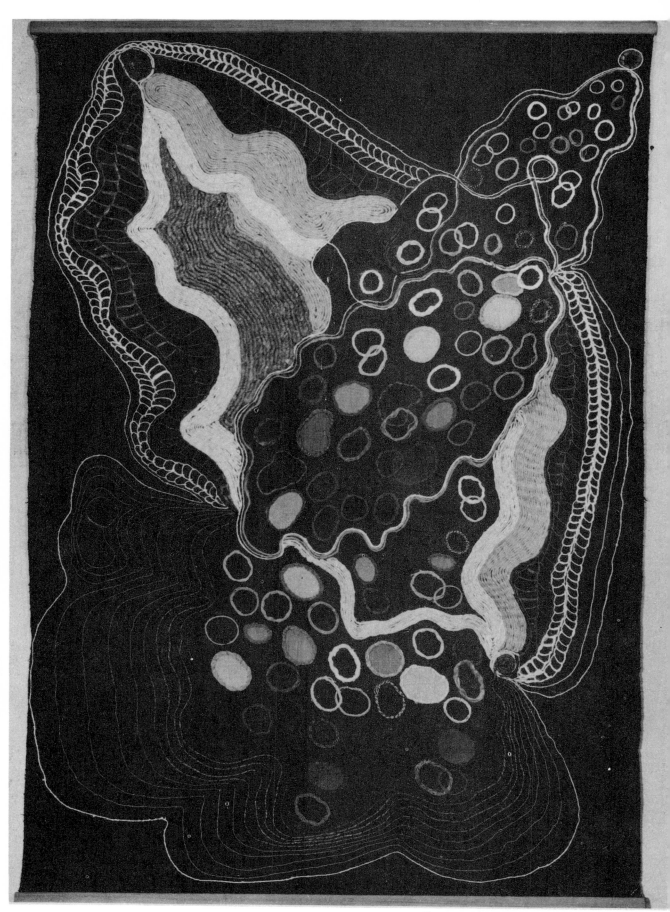

13. Dark Harbor *by Mariska Karasz*

An example of the couching stitch used for lines, fill-in, and shapes. Many varieties of yarns make the lines more interesting and rich in appearance.

1   stitchery

Embroidery and stitchery transmit basically the same meaning to the reader—that is, to arrange and combine various stitches to form a design or pattern in yarns, threads, and colors on a textile background. However, the term embroidery seems to convey the feeling of a more traditional art, such as crewelwork or cross-stitch, while stitchery gives a more contemporary and avant-garde impression. Actually it makes little difference what one calls this art, but what is meaningful is that the creative field of working with yarns and textiles has become a very important and active one in the past few years. It is no longer an art that is limited to the Sunday parlor and the folk artist, but one that is being practiced by leading designers around the world in an attempt to solve their artistic problems. As we have seen in the introduction, even the schoolchild has turned to this medium to express his everyday activities, his feelings, and his creative desires.

It is always difficult to determine where to classify some of the artists working in yarns and threads on textile backgrounds. Very often the contemporary designer includes many combined techniques in one artistic composition, and this presents the cataloguer with problems of correctly titling the medium. But this should not be our primary concern. Let us just say that those employing the traditional established sets of stitches are working in a more purely defined form of stitchery, whereas those combining other methods are "less pure." Those introducing a more extensive combination of approaches we will include in other areas. But again, in many cases, these people are using forms of stitchery, and generally we find them including a great amount of appliqué in their work.

Probably one of the persons most responsible for stimulating a rebirth of stitchery in the United States was Mariska Karasz. Miss Karasz carried embroidery far beyond what grandmother thought of as a method of decorating her chairbacks. She investigated instead any material that would fit through the eye of a needle and applied it to rich woolen textiles. She included other materials to complement her yarns and threads, such as paper and metals. Her experimentation took her far beyond the field of embroidery or stitchery, into the problems of painting with linens, cottons, shells, and other delightful materials. Miss Karasz had this to say about her work: "In planning a wall hanging, the material itself speaks by weight, by color and by texture. If the fabric background is humble, I use either elegant threads, or materials equally modest; if the length of wool is dull it may call for sparkle in the design. If the background is lustrous, it may be that the threads and yarns must be dull. Backgrounds are quite as important to the composition as the filaments applied to it. I prefer a neutral, fairly dark fabric that recedes—often of wool, sometimes of linen or silk." (*Craft Horizons*, April 1953, p.13) Although Miss Karasz has done stitchery on other objects besides wall hangings, her hangings are the pieces that have won her acclaim.

In Scandinavia the art of needlework has long been an important part of the lives of the people. As we saw in the Altarpiece of the Holar Church in Iceland, it reached a very high and disciplined level centuries ago. Today many artist-designers are engaged in various methods of textile design. One is Ulla Tollerz, who has employed stitchery techniques in the designs she sells to industry for reproduction. She is a young Swedish mother who spends her short free time in the art of stitchery. Although she also weaves, much of her work is done with needle and thread. Her work is delicate and feminine, and she often incorporates dainty glass beads along with cobbler threads and Japanese metallic thread (fig. 17). Her work has been highly rewarded with fellowships and grants to study in other European countries. One interesting facet of Mrs.

26

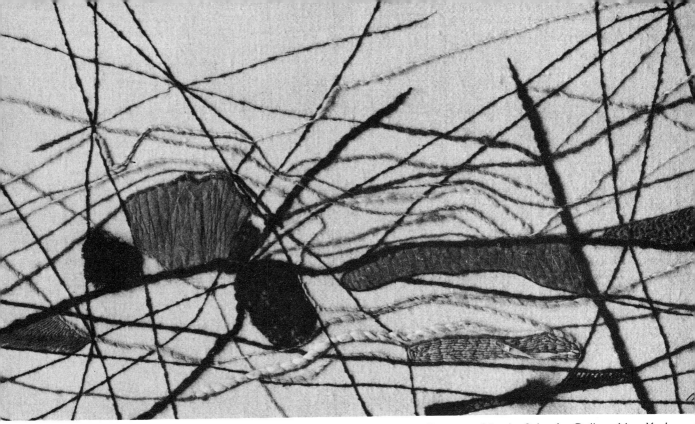

Courtesy of Bertha Schaefer Gallery, New York

4. Textural *by Mariska Karasz*
A network of yarns crossing and intersecting present a painting of depth and a feeling of an intricate web construction.

Tollerz' work is that it strikingly reflects her personality and character, and this is such an important element of the artist's work! From start to finish the product should be a creation pulled from the artist's own sources and experiences. A creative person never depends on the facilities of another person, but instead lets his development grow from his own individual interests, needs, and creative imagination.

In creating your first stitchery design, you might start out with simple wandering linear stitches, varying the widths and textures as you proceed across the background fabric and giving no thought to subject matter. Consider this a sample, and your debut with yarns, threads, and stitches. Cross over and under previous stitches until the fabric has been filled with texture and color. In few cases will this be an advanced design, but it will be exciting and exploratory. Your second step might be to use groups of stitches next to each other, like rocks on a countryside hill or patterns in a city. As you build this essay of texture, pattern, and color, vary the yarns and materials you apply. Don't be shy about your first few attempts, but

28   **15. Fair and Square** *by Mariska Karasz*

An interesting design of contrasts and repeated shapes gives the viewer a glimpse into the more complex stitches used by Miss Karasz. Photo by Jean Lange.

16. Sacrifice by Mariska Karasz

This is an excellent example of Mariska Karasz' approach to texture. As you can see, many threads and many sizes are combined in this geometric pattern.

Courtesy of Bertha Schaefer Gallery, New York

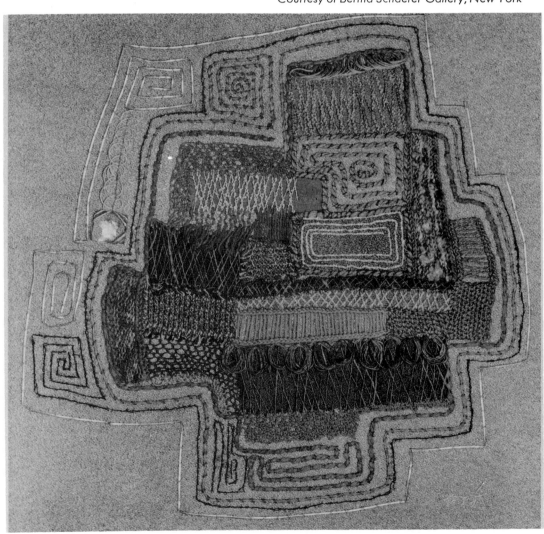

instead be bold and daring in color. Later you can begin to build a more determined and exacting combination of colors and yarns with better design qualities. Your first trials should be only experimental. Although you should always continue to investigate, your later pieces will be experimentation with a more knowledgeable background. Not only will you be technically more adept, with a wider familiarity with stitches, but you will also learn to express yourself more easily.

17. Sun In An Early Summer's Morning *by Ulla Tollerz*
Delicate sunbursts use beads and metallic threads in combination with stitchery to carry through a soft morning-dew atmosphere.

18. Stitchery Abstraction *by John Marko*
Bold stitches in this abstract work present the viewer with power and force. Simple yet strong, this piece of stitchery conveys a deep understanding of our contemporary design world.

From the author's collection

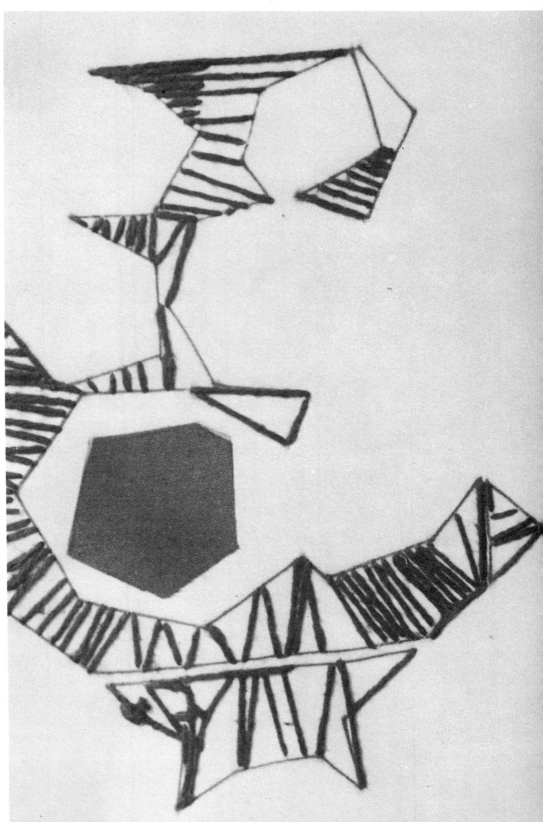

19. Architectural by Van Dommelen
Many stitches (couching, wave stitch, satin stitch, stem stitch, and others) are combined in this hanging. The more stitches used, the more interesting the design.

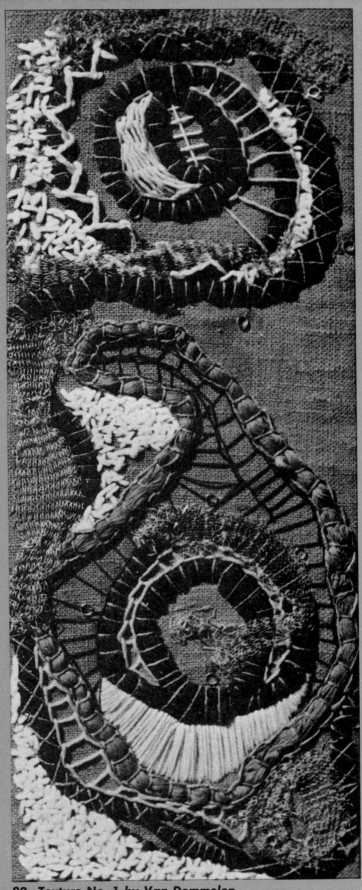

20. Texture No. 1 by Van Dommelen
Large and heavy groups of threads are couched with various
stitches to promote a deep, rich textural effect in this hanging.
A shell inspired the forms.

21. Blossoming Flower *by Van Dommelen*

This wall hanging was inspired by the stems, stamen, and seeds of a flower. The background for this piece was selected because it seemed to have the feeling of the earth in which flowers thrive.

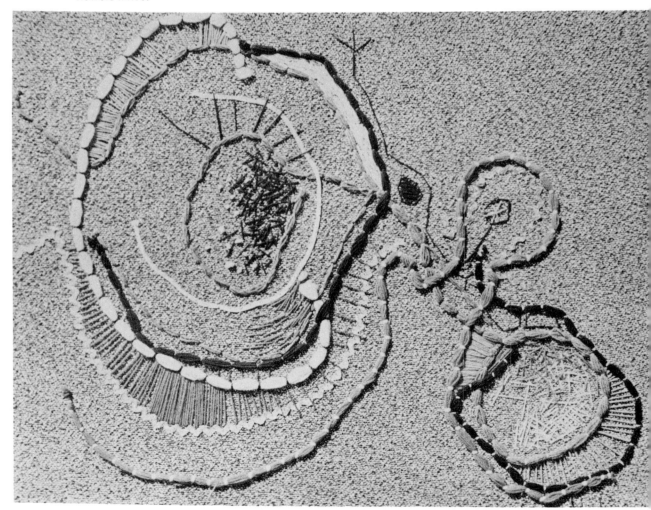

22. Desert Flower *by Van Dommelen*

Thread and yarn were used in this stitchery to give variety to the grasses. The background is burlap.

23. Metropolis *by Van Dommelen*

Open chain, ladder, and several combination stitches were used to convey the feeling of windows and floors in city buildings.

The beginner, especially the beginner who has had little contact with the art world, is very often at a loss for ideas and ways in which to express himself. However, this should not be extremely difficult in view of the fact that the individual lives in a fascinating place—the world. All that is necessary is to look around you, discover the environment in which you live. The city is full of shapes (fig. 19 and 23) and colors, and the countryside abounds with flowers, rocks, and weeds (fig. 21 and 22). Pick a subject—a scaffolding or a mushroom. Explore it and look at it. Investigate each line and curve. As you translate your subject into yarns and fabrics, it will at first seem mundane, but slowly it will develop a richness of pattern and texture that you have never noticed before. You will become much more intimate with this small part of the world than the spectator looking at your finished stitchery will ever be able to understand. Once you have made the first attempt, you will no longer be afraid to face other problems in your work.

There are literally hundreds of stitches available to the beginner who is interested in developing his stitch vocabulary. It would seem useless for this author to present them all in page after page of drawings and diagrams, for many writers have done this before. Although there is presented here a list of basic stitches with which you might begin to experiment, it is a good idea for you to wander by yourself for a while, inventing more individual approaches to your work.

After you have discovered that you can handle a needle and begin to find a good rapport between you and your yarns and fabrics, go to those sources that list in every fashion the myriad stitches available. The best place to find a logical type of grouping is in Mariska Karasz' book *Adventures in Stitches*, published by Funk & Wagnalls, which might be called a companion to this book. Miss Karasz has classified the stitches in many ways, giving many steps for each stitch. It is not easy to lose contact with her clear and concise manner of presentation. If, however, you are still a beginner, it would be advisable to start with the few basic stitches offered to you in this book.

24. Row 1: *Chain Stitch* After you have come up through the fabric, return the needle next to your first thread hole. Make a running stitch under the fabric with the needle; loop the thread under the needle and draw. Return the needle through the previous loop.

Row 2: *Open Chain Stitch* This stitch is the same as the Chain Stitch except that the needle reenters the fabric *apart* from the first thread hole. This can be varied in many ways as you experiment, but remember to keep the tension even.

Row 3: *Varied Stem Stitch* See Row 4.

Row 4: *Stem Stitch* Also called the Outline Stitch, this stitch can be varied as you work from left to right.

Row 5: *Satin Stitch* To be used in filling areas to be covered. Use single flat stitches, laying them close together. Be careful to keep the tension even.

Row 6: *French Knot* Bring the needle and thread completely through the background and wrap the thread around the needle several times (3-5) near where the thread comes out from the background. Return the needle through the fabric, pulling the needle and yarn through the wound threads.

Row 7: *Open Chain Couching* Use the Open Chain Stitch to attach large cords and threads to the surface of a fabric (See Row 2, Fig. 25.)

Row 8: *Seed Stitch* The Seed Stitch is an excellent stitch to utilize when a filled-in area is desired. This stitch is simple and uncomplicated. Use small, large, or a combination of different size stitches for a more interesting effect. The stitches can be made in any direction, close or compact. These stitches can also be piled on top of each other to make a thick texture.

Row 9: *Blanket or Buttonhole Stitch* After pulling the yarn through the background, insert the needle at a 45° angle to the line of work. Make a running stitch under the fabric straight back to the line of work and loop the thread under the needle. Pull the yarn through and begin the next stitch.

Row 10: *Feather Stitch* This stitch is a relative of the Blanket Stitch. Instead of the running stitch under the fabric being perpendicular, it is slanted.

Row 11 *Double Feather Stitch* This is the Feather Stitch worked on both sides of the line of work alternately.

Row 12: *Herringbone Stitch* After coming through the fabric, make a 45° stitch. Backstitch and cross over your first stitch. Now backstitch again, crossing over your last stitch. Repeat this as you continue on parallel work lines. Vary for interest if desired.

Row 13 *Combination Stitch* Open Chain Stitch and Chain Stitch have been combined to make this unusual stitch. Any stitches you learn can be combined for effects you might wish.

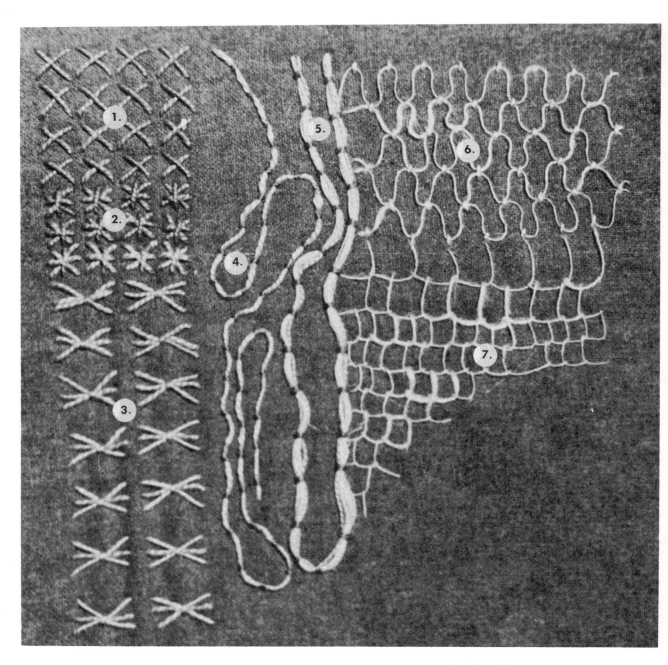

25. Row 1: *Cross-stitch* An old American stitch which is closely related to the Herringbone except that each cross is independent of the others. Instead of backstitching after the crossing, the thread makes a small running stitch under the fabric and begins again.

Row 2: *Double Cross-stitch* This is a Cross-stitch with another Cross-stitch laid on top.

Row 3: *Sheaf Filling* Three or more parallel stitches held down with one or more simple Couching Stitches pulled in at the center.

Row 4: *Couching* Couching is a simple stitch. Lay one thread on the surface of the fabric and sew it down with small stitches of another thread.

Row 5: *Group Couching* This is the same as plain Couching except that more than one thread is laid on the fabric before attaching to the surface.

Row 6: *Cloud Filling* After making several rows of small vertical running stitches, work another thread back and forth between the parallel lines of running stitches. Keep the tension loose if you want a curved effect to the stitch.

Row 7: *Buttonhole Filling* This is the same as the Buttonhole Stitch except that the artist connects each row into the heading of the previous row.

38

26. *Sampler of Stitches*

1. Chain Stitch	3. Sheaf Filling	6. Buttonhole Filling	9. French Knots
2. Couching	4. Herringbone Stitch	7. Open Chain Couching	10. Feather Stitch
	5. Open Chain Stitch	8. Blanket Stitch	11. Stem Stitch

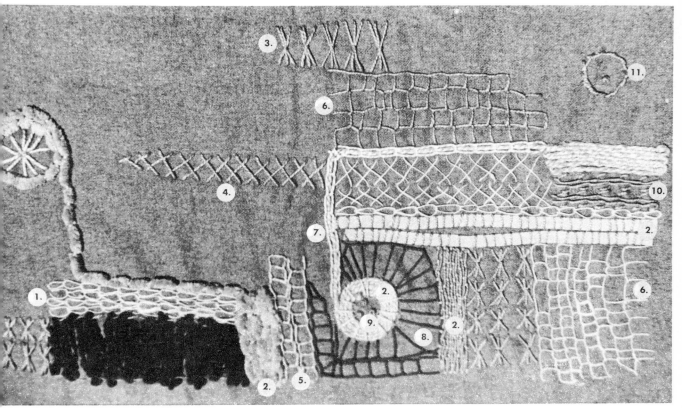

2 appliqué

27. Adam's Half *by Jean Ray Laury*
Tiny, meticulous stitches have been used to appliqué this interesting nature study to the background. Photo by Frank B. Laury.

2   appliqué

We have seen stitchery and the variety of effects that can be obtained from such a versatile art medium. The combination of many stitches to achieve a valid and profound painting in yarns is only one of the many methods of constructing and creating a decorative wall hanging. Appliqué, the process of fastening cutout pieces of fabric onto a background of fabric, is another means of producing interesting results in creative textile design.

Appliqué is not a new method of working. The folk artist has been using appliqué for hundreds of years, and we can see much of what was done by our pioneer peoples in the many museum collections of American folk art.

Although appliqué might appear to be a limited area in which to work, this is not true. An artist's only limitation is the extent of his or her imagination and creative stimulus. Once one begins to have a vocabulary of stitches, appliqué becomes a thousand times more interesting and intriguing. There are many combinations of interesting textiles and yarns (or threads) that can be used. One need not limit oneself. The forms and shapes one uses will open completely new horizons for experimentation. As we saw in the chapter on stitchery, there are many sources that can be used as inspirations for design.

HAND APPLIQUÉ

The hand method of appliqué is a manner of working which immediately strikes the craftsman as challenging and full of depth, and leaves the executor full of pride and accomplishment.

When looking at an appliqué executed by a contemporary such as Jean Ray Laury, one is immediately reminded of the work done by the San Blas Indians. Mrs. Laury's pieces are intricate, fine, and delicate wall hangings that have a beautifully fresh quality and are very strongly reminiscent of our American tradition. Her work illustrates how the modern artist has maintained a meticulous standard of work and craftsmanship (fig. 30). Mrs. Laury feels that craftsmanship is a most important part of an artist's work, and that one should not spoil the final beauty through sloppiness and effects that are too novel. Her designs are derived from nature, and the colors she uses are suggested to her by her subject matter. She often applies the pieces to her fabric background with small running stitches, and these stitches become incorporated as decorative lines to enhance the form she is expressing. Both wall hangings, "Pods: A Pair" (fig. 28) and "Adam's Half" (fig. 27), illustrated in this chapter are good examples of her approach to creative personal expression through hand appliqué methods.

Just the opposite in execution, but still remaining on a level of excellence in production, are Marilyn Pappas' wall hangings (fig. 31 and 32); her work shows a freedom and spontaneity in applying thread and materials. She obtains a feeling of casual application, so that her finished product makes one think immediately of the abstract expressionist painter and his profound understanding of the artistic statement. Mrs. Pappas does not use a large range of thread, but her invention of forms is unlimited, along with the combination of colors that she utilizes. Mrs. Pappas also uses a great quantity of interesting fabrics that she obtains from shops in her vicinity selling remnants and mill-ends. These are available at very low prices and afford the artist a larger selection of working materials.

In hand appliqué methods, the artist can approach the medium in different ways. Mrs. Laury's work illustrates the method of turning under the edges, making fine and determined hems. One must face the task of a long and tedious job, because small, even, tiny stitches are incorporated in this part of the work. The end result is a product

44

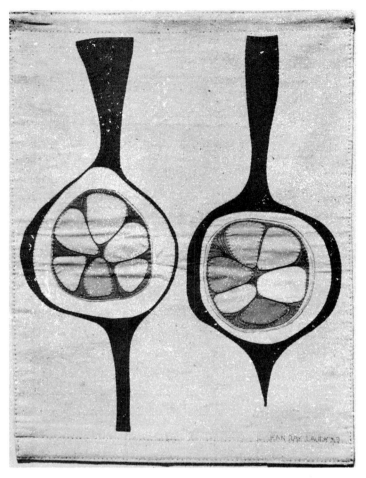

28. Pods: A Pair *by Jean Ray Laury*
Two large simple shapes play an important role in conveying the subject matter of seeds and pods in this hanging. Photo by Tom Hurley.

that is carefully delineated, with forms clearly designated. However, work done in the style of Mrs. Pappas gives an entirely different feeling. Her edges are unturned and loose, and her stitches seem to be more experimental types. Certainly the viewer can see at once that Mrs. Pappas seldom follows a dictionary of stitches. Still, both have aimed at the same goal—that of creatively expressing emotions and ideas in design on fabrics.

29. Sapling *by Jean Ray Laury*
Simplicity is often a deciding factor in a successful design. Photo by Tom Hurley.

30. Homing Tree *by Jean Ray Laury*
A contemporary approach rings through this hanging, which shows a deep understanding of an old American craft, pure appliqué. Photo by Frank B. Laury.

31. The Great Beach *by Marilyn Pappas*
A medley of interesting textures held in place by hundreds of stitches is the essence of this contemporary abstract wall hanging.

32. Still Life With Table *by Marilyn Pappas*
Unhemmed edges and seemingly casual appliqué characterize Mrs. Pappas' approach to a combination of appliqué and stitchery.

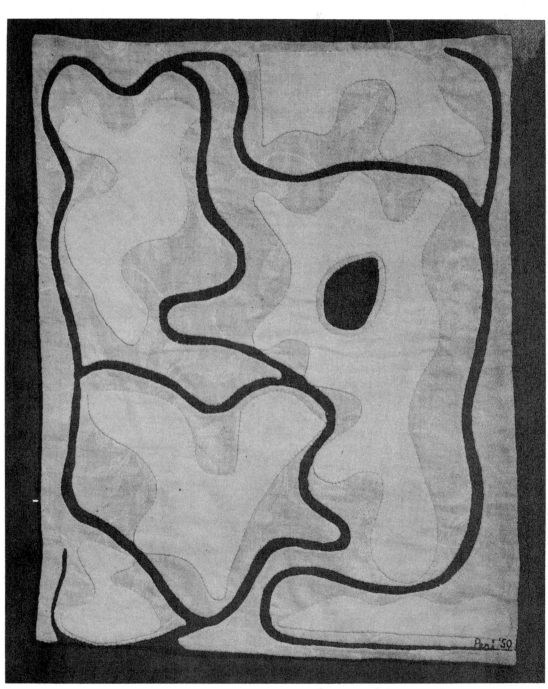

33. Appliqué *by Eve Peri*
This hanging uses cotton and linen in an unusual composition of line and shape. Photo by Charles Uht.

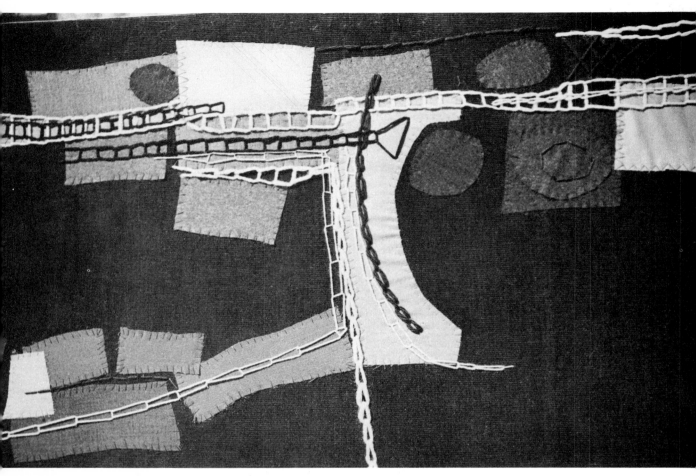

34. Blue Landscape *by Van Dommelen*

A landscape inspired by an aerial view of the passing world is executed in a combination of chain stitches and simple unhemmed appliquéd pieces.

35. Appliqué *by Bruno Romeda*

Interestingly textured backgrounds of squares and re¢tangles are used for the simply cut familiar shapes of this appliquéd hanging.

Courtesy of American Craftsmen's Council

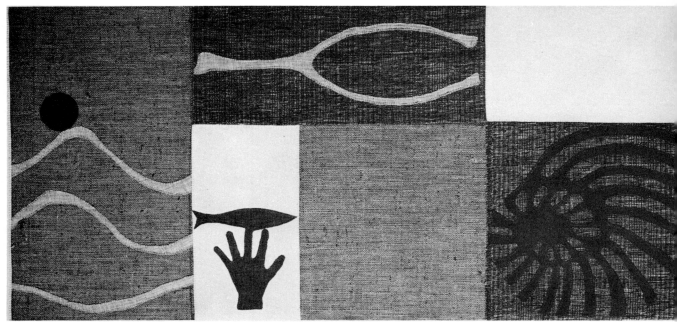

MACHINE APPLIQUE

While the hand method of appliqué is familiar to most of us, the use of machine appliqué in wall hangings is new and different. Because we live in an age of technology, the machine plays an important part in the homes of all Americans; so far it has seldom, however, contributed to the esthetic side of our lives. But in the new zigzag sewing machine we have an instrument that is both a tool of utilitarian value and a tool of art. Through this completely automatic machine, we can obtain artistic results that are for the most part as yet undiscovered. Stitches that are predetermined for the operator; stitches that can be invented by widening, lengthening, and doubling; and a stitch that has the freedom of a pencil line are all available. However, even the small portable machine can be used extremely successfully in creative wall-hanging execution. It is not necessary to own a large or expensive sewing machine, but, of course, such a machine is more versatile.

Working on a machine can be highly experimental and great fun. The operator can couch on heavy cards (fig. 42) through the use of selected stitches, or can use a variety of threads in the bobbin. Fabrics can be appliquéd onto the background fabric merely by loosening the feeder foot and freely pushing the fabric back and forth under the needle, as in darning; even the simplest machine can be used for this process. If the operator wishes, he can be more exacting and use an embroidery hoop for various types of stitches as he works out the design. The fabrics can be appliquéd without hemming the edges by using a thick appliqué stitch, or one can revert to the older method of hemming the edges first.

In working with the machine, it is wise to begin by cutting out many interesting shapes of different textures and colors, as you can see had been done in Fig. 37. Next place them on the background fabric, making sure that the fabric is a strong and stable one. The background fabric in "Flowers" is white duck and the fabric used in "Blue Night" (fig. 40) is a heavy denim. If the background fabric is not a good healthy textile, the possibility of puckering is very high. When a weak fabric is used, incorporate two pieces to help to eliminate puckering. "Menorah" (fig. 44) was sewn on a very slithery rayon fabric and several pieces were sandwiched together to form a solid and substantial backing. Pin the shapes and forms onto the background (see fig. 41), and then appliqué the pieces

54

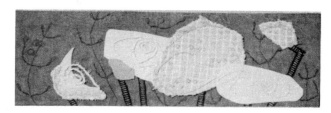

36. Sunflowers *by Miriam McGrew*
Appliquéd sunflowers on top of black organdy with stitchery underneath—an entirely different approach to the same subject that Frances Robinson used in Fig. 43.

with the machine. Or you can roll the loose, cut pieces, without pinning, into a tight roll and work directly under the needle, unrolling the fabric as the unsewn pieces are reached in the roll. This is a more difficult method, but it does eliminate the pinning step. Other fabrics can be laid on top for more effects. Organdy and other transparent fabrics are interesting to overlay, because the artist can mix colors, much as an artist can do with paint (fig. 37). You can continue to overlay fabrics until the desired effect is reached. Netting, lace, and theatrical gauze are fun to incorporate also. Yarns can then be couched on by using a couching stitch with the machine, or the yarns can be added by hand, using some of the stitches introduced in the stitchery chapter. In Fig. 11, the author combined the two techniques. As you will discover in a later chapter, there are certainly no rules established concerning the combinations of various methods of working. In fact, the results are often more distinctive when methods are mixed. Some of the most interesting textural combinations are achieved when a flat machine-applied piece of fabric is nested close to a thick basket-weave stitch done by hand.

There are only a few who use the machine continually as a medium for creative expression. Several European craftsmen utilize its potentialities, but even fewer artists in the United States have discovered it and made any progress with the possibilities it offers. Besides the author, Frances Robinson is constantly exploring this new approach to wall-hanging design. Her work has been widely acclaimed, and she has contributed to many important exhibitions in the craft world. Miss Robinson mixes threads of different colors (fig. 43), and her hangings are fabrics covered with hundreds of small lines carefully placed next to each other. This is reminiscent

37. Flowers *by Van Dommelen*

A combination of cottons and organdy appliquéd by the sewing machine gives transparent qualities to this hanging.

38. Rocks and Roots *by Van Dommelen*
  The use of upholstery as backing fabric offers a startling likeness of the stratified levels of the earth. The contemporary artist enjoys viewing his subject in new and unique ways.

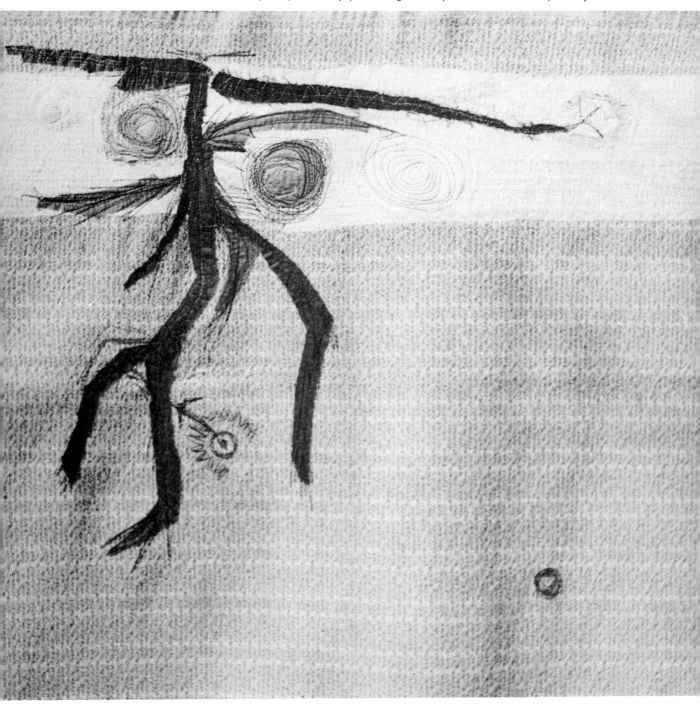

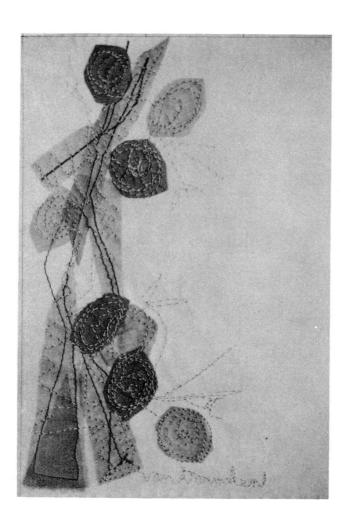

39. Rocks Vertical *by Van Dommelen*
A small wall hanging showing the use of the sewing machine as an appliqué tool.

58

of what the impressionists did with pointillism in the late 19th century, when they used, for example, thousands of tiny red and blue dots and ended with a purple field of color. Her work has a luminous quality that results from overlapping these stitched areas, which produces sparkling transparent color effects. She deals with subject matter that is easily understood, and uses a painting approach which is contemporary and modern.

You can slowly begin to experiment with the sewing machine as your art instrument, until it has become as creative to you as a brush is to the ordinary painter. This will not mean that you are working with a medium that is less valid, but only that you have opened up another field of creative development in today's art world. It is important not to let the machine dictate or be the thinker for you. Instead, you must master the machine and guide it toward a more creative approach in your search for new forms.

With the machine today, yarns can be appliquéd as well as other materials. Again, as in stitchery and hand appliqué, only your imagination limits the use of the machine. What is really wonderful about the machine is the way it lends itself to spontaneity and creative experimentation. When working by hand, the piece in question very often becomes overworked and dull in its painstaking detail, but the machine seems to keep the idea fresh and invigorating. It is possible to work very much faster, enabling you to keep alive the original inspiration which prompted you to begin the work.

The creative uses of the machine have not been taken advantage of in most of our schools. This is an excellent instrument to explore more fully in home economics classes in high schools across the nation. This might mean the elimination of apron-making, but much more meaningful results could be achieved.

40. Blue Night *by Van Dommelen*
Many swatches of old fabric are utilized in this blue composition.

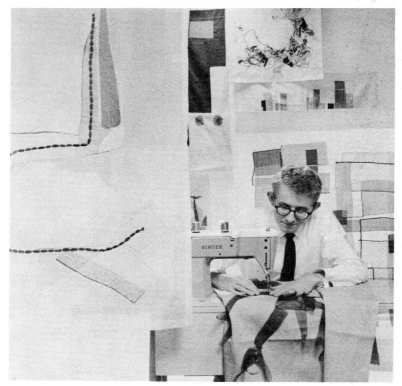

41. Author Working on Wall Hanging
A view of the author working on the sewing machine surrounded by
pieces of his work. *Look* Photo.

60

42. The machine can do many things for the craftsman. Here we see the
machine couching a heavy yarn onto a wall hanging.

43. Sunflowers *by Frances Robinson*
Miss Robinson is one of the few artists working with the machine as a tool to express art forms.

Museum of Contemporary Crafts

44. Menorah *by Van Dommelen*
Religious subject matter can be beautifully executed with the sewing machine. Photo by Jean Lange.

Montclair Art Museum, Montclair, New Jersey

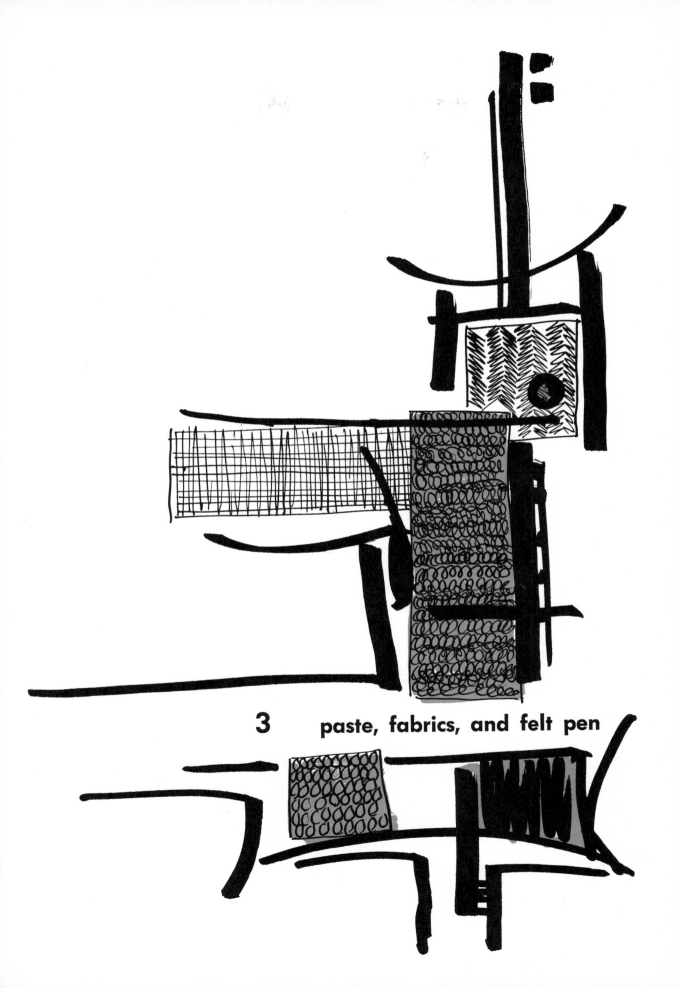

3   paste, fabrics, and felt pen

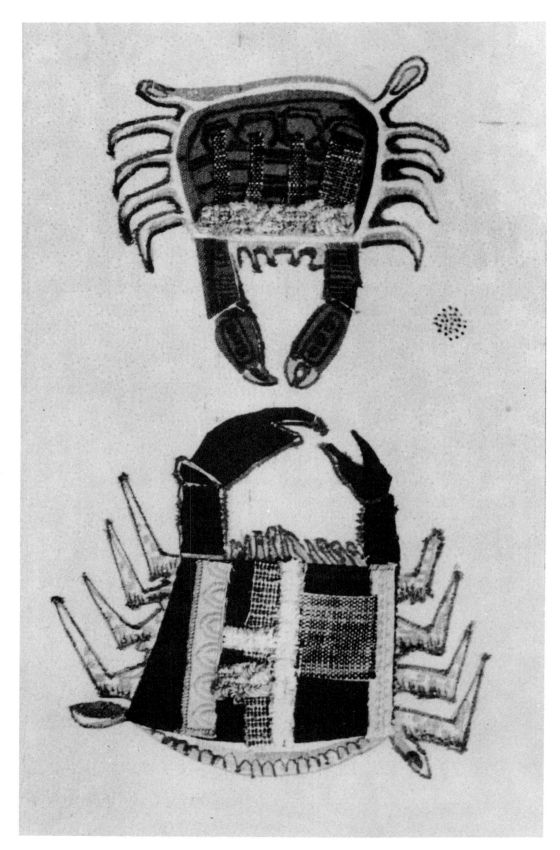

45. The Crabs *by John Marko*   *From the author's collection*
A view into sea life through fabric, paste, and felt pen.

3   paste, fabrics, and felt pen

Using paste, fabric, and felt pens is a relatively uncomplicated method of constructing a wall hanging; you as a beginner can easily grasp the full impact, versatility, and spontaneous possibilities of this medium.

Although this particular medium cannot be guaranteed as a highly durable type of work, we know that paste and materials have been used for many years. The cubists in France were extremely experimental in this area during the first part of the twentieth century, and the objects they created are still extant for us to study. In a later chapter, we will look more closely at the collage work the cubists achieved.

Because we have seen other artists use this method, we can assume that our attempts with fabric can be just as lasting, and, at the same time, just as vital as those art forms in which Picasso, Braque, and Gris worked.

You must realize, however, that this medium must be limited to wall-hanging design. Several other creative techniques examined in this book could easily be applied to various household uses, but employing this technique for anything but nonutilitarian objects would be disastrous, for repeated washing and dry-cleaning will obviously ruin a collage hanging.

But because few materials are necessary to create and finish a wall hanging of this nature, the beginner as well as the advanced student can become extremely versatile and experimental without overstepping a limited budget. (See Chapter Eleven).

It is important to stretch the background material on a good strong board. This is recommended because of the unpliable nature of paste after the wall hanging is completed. The stretching can be accomplished as recommended in Chapter Ten; however, it is possible simply to glue the background fabric to the board that you will be using as the permanent stretcher. Using this method gives you assurance that the piece will remain rigid. From here on you can simply lay the small cut pieces of fabric and material against the background according to your preconceived sketch, or in a spontaneous manner without a sketch. Approaching the problem without a sketch is much more exciting to the creator, and he can solve the problems as he is confronted with them in the growth of the composition. Undesirable elements of the design are easily covered by applying more pieces of fabric onto the previously pasted materials. At the same time this step will bring about a three-dimensional quality to the work that is interesting and exciting.

Almost any type of fabric may be used, so long as it is strong and heavy enough to retain the glue on the reverse or underside. Carefully consider materials that are delicate and open in weave before incorporating them into your hanging. Silks, light cottons, and marquisettes obviously would permit glues to penetrate to the surface and leave unwanted (in most cases) stains. Heavy ducks and drills are well suited to use as background fabrics. Wools, heavy denims, and sturdy linens are good choices for applied pieces, and Elmer's Glue-All serves adequately as the adhesive.

The felt pen can be used throughout the procedure. There is no rule that the lines made with the pen should be added at any certain point in the process. In fact, the finished product will be more successful if it has ink lines disappearing under various pieces of the pasted fabrics. Remember that the felt pen is an active instrument, and that the ink begins to color the fabric as soon as it has been placed on its surface. Slowly (sometimes quickly) the ink penetrates the fabric, giving interesting blending and bleeding qualities. The harder you press down on the pen, the darker the line becomes; the lighter you press, the more sketchy the effects will be.

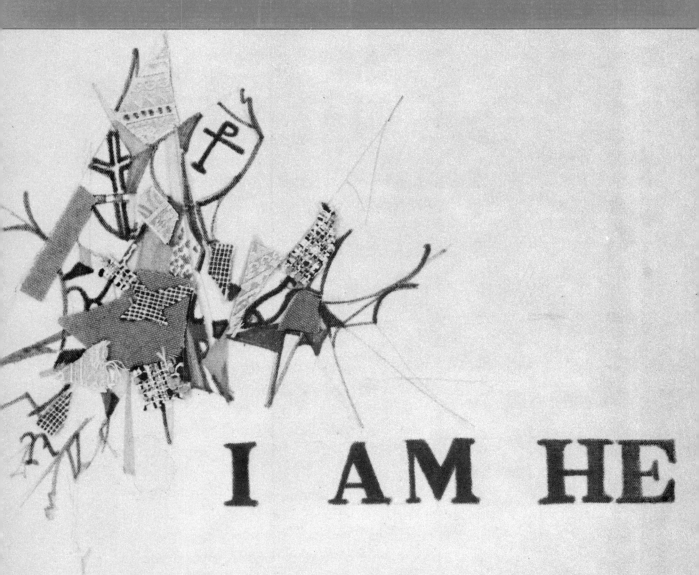

I AM HE

46. I Am He by John Marko
An abstract structure showing uses of fabric, paste, and felt pen to illustrate a philosophic statement by the artist.

The felt pen contains a waterproof ink, and is therefore not removable after it has been applied. Do some preliminary drawing first or be extremely sure of your plan, for unless you are an accomplished artist, you will find mistakes difficult to cover.

When you apply the fabric, make sure you incorporate a variety of edges. Don't cut all the pieces carefully around the edges. Let some of them fray for textural effects, because these raw edges can be glued down at a later time in the work. Pinking shears may also be used for interesting edge effects. However, if you would like a meticulous composition, like the style or approach Jean Ray Laury uses in appliqué, you may achieve this by carefully cutting and trimming the raw edges.

In John Marko's work "The Crabs" (fig. 45), you can see the interesting use of fabrics and different depths of texture. Some of the shapes are clean-cut, and others seem to have a rough and loose feeling. The various weaves of some fabrics will dictate many of the effects you achieve; let those involuntary things happen. There are times when mistakes aid in making your design more successful, and often you can build on these mistakes. This should apply to all work and media mentioned in this book. Mistakes are not necessarily bad, but instead open up, in many cases, a new outlook or approach to the composition you are creating.

This author, however, feels that no composition should be made up entirely of chance happenings. Instead, you should analyze your composition intellectually as you continue to work. Stop at regular intervals and view your work from a distance before proceeding to another layer of fabric. Before a new piece of fabric is permanently placed on the design, you should have a determined and substantial knowledge of what this new addition will do to the overall composition. If necessary, lay aside your work and start on a new hanging. Having several compositions going at the same time stimulates the mind and keeps you in constant activity.

Paste and fabric are wonderful materials to incorporate into the elementary school art program. Although this medium is an extremely vigorous and rewarding one for adults, the possibilities for young children are practically unlimited. Children of all ages become very excited with the use of scissors and paste. Working with fabrics and paste will offer them the chance to experience textures in visual and tactile experiments. They will have the opportunity to learn about colors and will find wonderful possibilities for creative work, but, most important, they will be taking part in an activity that will develop their own sensitivities and growth. An understanding and awareness of their individual abilities will grow as they manipulate the materials.

47. Horizontal Construction *by Van Dommelen*
Paste, fabric, and felt pen wall hanging on a duck fabric background.

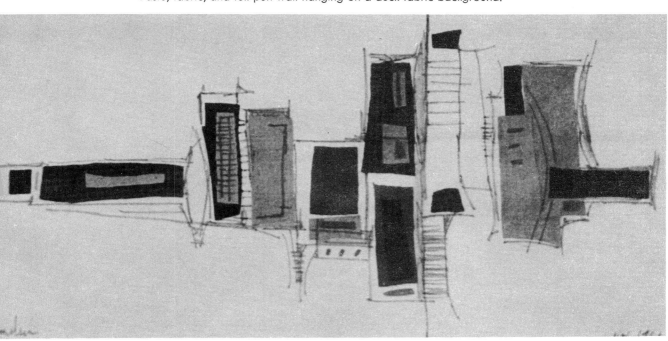

48. Xat #1 *by Van Dommelen*

70

49. Xat #1, detail

50. The Beach *by Van Dommelen*
Burlap, linen, and wool pasted on a duck fabric background, using felt pen drawing super-imposed on the pasted fabric.

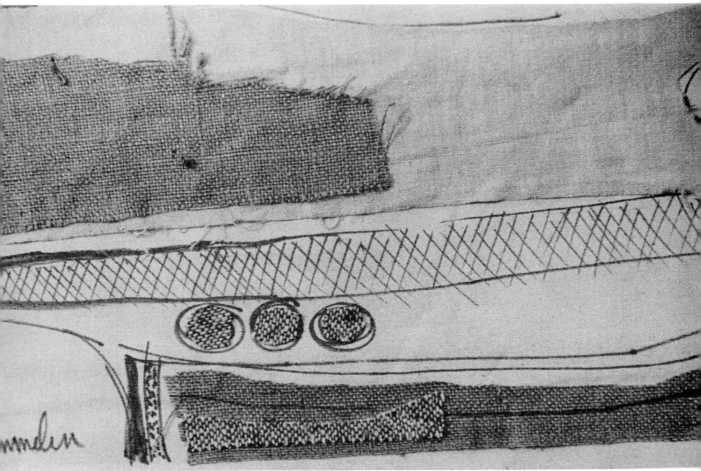

4 press-on tape and felt pen

51. Abstraction of A Violin *by Van Dommelen*
A simple hanging using only press-on tape. The composition is not unique, but the medium is an innovation.

4   press-on tape and felt pen

Every mother is acquainted with the problems of repairing the familiar "holey" pair of pants that her son wears home from his excursions into the woods and over the barbed fence into the vacant field. Few housewives, however, are aware of the beauty they are able to create with the small strips of press-on tape they use to patch their children's clothing.

Obviously, press-on tape and felt pen are ideally suited to the woman at home who would like to make decorative objects to enrich her family's surroundings. Of course, this is also a good medium for high school and college students. It is worth attempting in both home and school, but it seems to me that the woman alone at home has materials at her fingertips for this type of creative work. It is not adaptable for use in elementary schools because of the danger involved in the handling of electric irons.

Press-on tape can be used by itself very successfully, but using a felt marker or pen with it adds a great deal of character to the wall hanging. The problem of using the tape by itself is that it tends to look stylized and sterile. However, when it is used with a felt pen or marker, one can achieve many more interesting effects. When the craftsman finds it tedious to cut many thin pieces of the tape, he can easily substitute marks he can draw with the felt pen.

Very small hangings, such as the series presented in this chapter, can be created with few materials. All the hangings in this group measure from 6" x 9" to 8" x 11". They were made on felt pieces obtained in a fabric shop, and then mounted on cotton backgrounds. Their usefulness is unlimited—from decoration in the child's bedroom to a grouping on the living room wall. A series could be hung in the kitchen, or in a small uninteresting hall which needs color to enliven its gloomy atmosphere.

It is also not impossible to use stitchery along with tape. The only difficulty seems to be with the mechanics of pulling the yarns and threads through the tape. This process often causes the tape to be pulled off the background fabric. But still there are excellent ways of combining the two materials. As you can see in Fig. 52, titled "Red Dot," press-on tape has been combined with regular sewing thread. The tape has been cut in abstract shapes that are combined to achieve an Oriental flavor, and thread stitchery has been added to soften the overly clean and rigid lines that the press-on tape often produces. The same softening of these harsh edges can take place when the magic marker or felt pen is used.

There is no reason why press-on tape cannot be combined with methods discussed in Chapter Three concerning Paste, Fabrics, and Felt Pen. In fact, using only press-on tape tends to give the hanging a flat appearance, and by adding unusual textures you can bring more interesting depth, pattern, and color into the piece you are designing.

The beginner who has difficulty in designing (even after attempts in stitchery and appliqué) might start out in this chapter with basic shapes that are familiar to everyone. It is not necessary to begin with concrete subject matter; however, those things we visualize in our close surroundings seem more natural to us.

Triangles, as illustrated in Fig. 53, are easy to arrange in networks of construction. The artist is able to achieve a sense of depth and space, as well as a design that moves from one area of the fabric to another. Imagine a piece of drapery fabric designed in the same manner. It could add a rich pattern to a room that is dull and in need of sparkle. Because press-on tape can be laundered and dry-cleaned, this technique can be used to add decorative elements to utilitarian household pieces.

In contrast to the structural effect of "Composition In Triangles,"

"Composition In Circles" (fig. 54) seems more related to the organic and to the natural world. But these basic forms can also be found stimulating and worthy of investigation. The overlapping of forms and lines is usually a more dynamic solution to design than is the use of isolated shapes. Although this is not always true, superimposing one shape on another will generally aid in making the composition stronger. Look around your surroundings, and you will discover many images of superimposed objects. Take a walk and study the many simple forms, lines, and shapes that are dependent on each other in some way.

A look into the machinery of our modern world might impress you with other shapes and forms. Here squares and rectangles could be the stimulating source for your composition, as in Figs. 55 and 56.

Regardless of where you look, the world you live in and the experiences you have in that world will be the influencing factors in the designing you do. As your experiences multiply and the visual world stimulates you more and more, your activities in design will constantly change into more meaningful forms. The alert artist cannot ignore the universe and the world in which he creates—because he is the world and universe.

52. Red Dot *by Van Dommelen*
A combination of press-on tape and thread stitchery provides an interesting method of working.

53. Composition In Triangles *by Van Dommelen*
Simple triangles make up the shapes in this composition with press-on tape and felt pen.

54. Composition In Circles *by Van Dommelen*
Circles reminiscent of flowers, rocks, or mushrooms are used to complete this design.

55. Composition In Rectangles *by Van Dommelen*

56. Composition In White And Black Squares *by Van Dommelen*

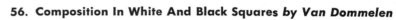

80

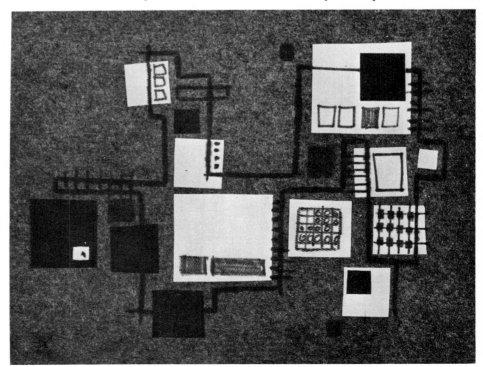

57. Composition Of Flowers *by Van Dommelen*

81

58. Violin And Guitar *by Pablo Picasso*
Pasted cloth, oil, pencil, and plaster on canvas were used as a means of expression by
Picasso in the year 1913. This is only one example of the many experiments that he conducted
in pasted collage.

5 paper, collage, and fabrics

For centuries, paper has been used as a background for artistic expression. It has had almost every conceivable thing done to it; we even hear that clothing is being constructed of paper. It is therefore not so surprising to learn that paper may be used in the making of decorative wall hangings.

An artist of our time who discovered new horizons in the creative use of paper is Pablo Picasso. He pasted paper, drew on paper, painted on paper—including newspaper (fig. 58). In the year 1913, Picasso was deep in the midst of his cubist period, and during this time he did many studies with various combinations of paper and other materials. He often used paper in his oil paintings, and he incorporated much newspaper with his India ink drawings. These pieces are still in excellent condition, and can be seen today in the A.E. Gallatin Collection at the Philadelphia Museum of Art (fig. 59).

But Picasso was not the only established artist who utilized paper for creative experimentation. Many artists turned to collage as a means of expressing their ideas. In 1937, Jean (Hans) Arp used torn paper (fig. 60) along with India ink washes as a means of making his creative statements. Arp also used stitchery as a form of painting in his "Dancer" (fig. 61), in which a simple couched stitch forms a rhythmical dancing form. If we were to look further into the archives of art history, we would find that Paul Klee, the Swiss artist, was a great protagonist of unusual paper usage in art.

85

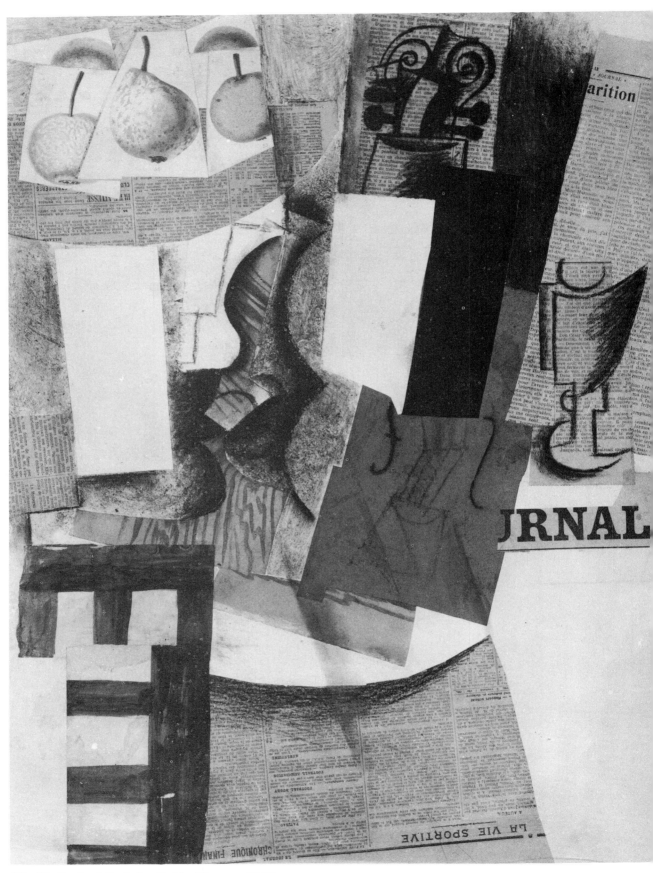

59. Violin And Fruit *by Pablo Picasso, 1913*
Charcoal and pasted papers were used in free experimentation by Picasso at the turn of the century.

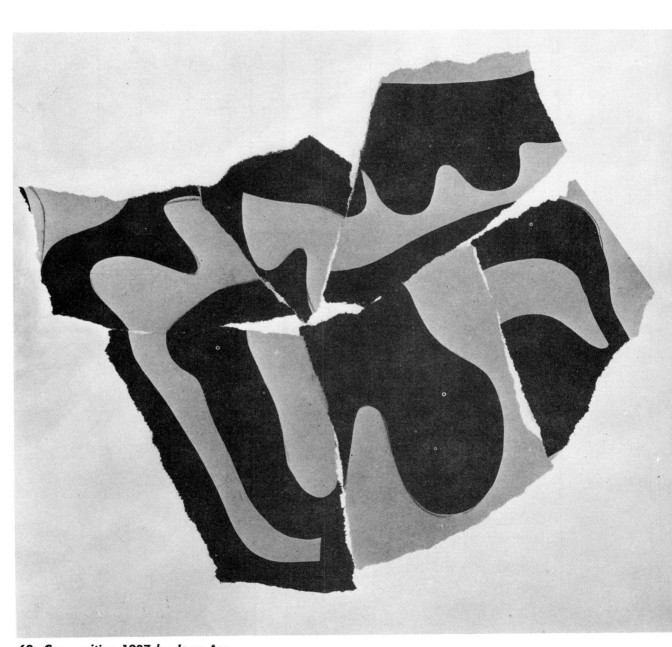

60. Composition 1937 *by Jean Arp*

An example of torn paper with India ink wash collage that expresses the height of simplicity in calm images. Arp developed the collage to a high degree of sensitivity in the 1930's.

A. E. Gallatin Collection, Philadelphia Museum of Art

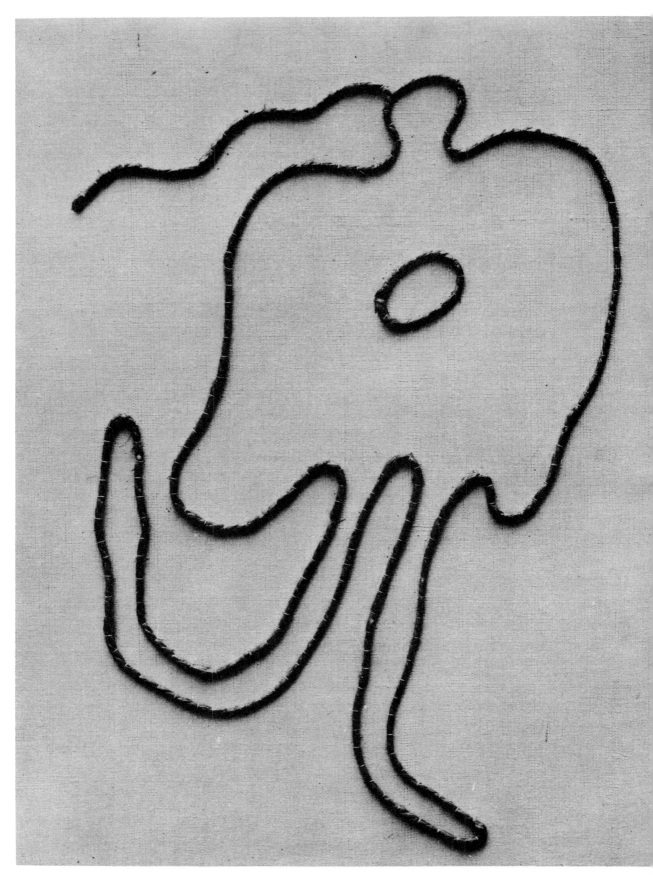

61. Dancer *by Jean Arp*
  One would hardly imagine a painter using stitchery in his work, but Arp did just that. A simple couched stitch portrays the rythmic movements of the dance.

Courtesy of Sidney Janis Gallery, New York

Our main interest in paper here is its function as a wall-hanging medium. At this point, we might notice that it is difficult to determine the line between wall hangings and collage work, because wall hangings at times become nothing more than collage executions.

Paper is a delicate material to work with; after years of exposure to sun, air, and humidity, it yellows and weakens. It is, therefore, often necessary to frame this type of work under glass. It is then easy to question its validity as a hanging as opposed to a painting in "fine art." But it would probably be best to leave this problem for the art historians to ponder. We are more interested in creating than in classifying objects.

There are many ways of working with paper and fabric. The author finds this method highly satisfactory for sketching with fabrics: using a strong paper as a background, small pieces of cut fabric are pasted on with a good, strong glue, such as Elmer's Glue-All, and India ink is brushed or penned over the top for linear effects. The artist can also use a felt pen, if this is preferred to India ink. The effects are similar, and both are quick answers to sketching problems for the wall-hanging designer. Water color can be incorporated as well.

As Mariska Karasz demonstrated in her work, paper can be used directly on the surface of a fabric background. This can be accomplished by large overlapping stitches that do not necessarily puncture the paper, but only hold it in place. In "Textural Stripes" (fig. 62), various paper strips have been couched onto a woolen fabric background for a collage-type hanging. The sewing machine has been used to add other textural effects to the composition.

Metallic foils can also be included in a hanging in which this method is used. With this step, the area of three-dimensional work, which we will discuss at greater length in Chapter Nine, is approached.

Another method of using paper and fabric is to stitch directly onto a paper background (fig. 63). This can be a delicate operation, since paper is torn very easily by tension. This means that you must select a strong paper or cardboard for the background, and pull the thread through the paper gently and not too tightly. Fabrics can be appliquéd, and other papers can be applied in interesting patterns of texture and color.

At once we can see that this could be an area of art expression for many groups. Elementary school children, as well as older pupils, could easily adopt this type of work. University students can experiment with this technique with great satisfaction and excitement. It is not limiting in any way, but can open up a wide field of creative endeavors.

The finished art expression can be mounted in a frame, or hung on a dowel as the Chinese and Japanese do with their lovely Oriental scrolls.

Fabric can be stretched on a frame before the work begins, or this can be done later—depending on the abilities and desires of the craftsman.

As you can well imagine, it is impossible to list all the many possibilities of this collage approach to making wall hangings. Remember, too, that it is one of the least expensive methods of working. Any student, teacher, or homemaker has the "makings" for a collage wall handing at his or her immediate call. No unusual materials are needed, yet this is one of the most rewarding and creative art forms available today.

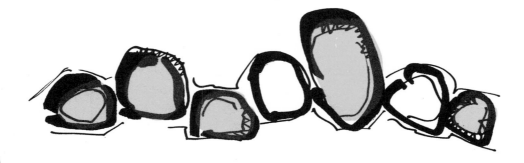

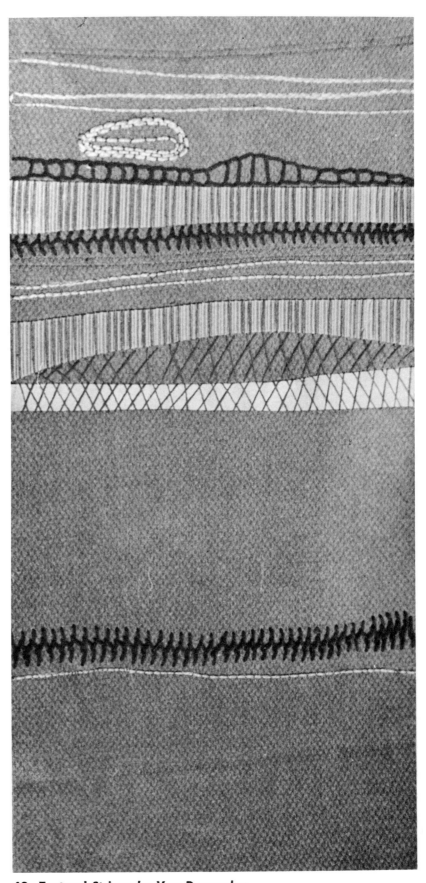

62. Textural Stripes *by Van Dommelen*
A sampler using paper, fabric, stitchery, and appliqué makes an interesting textural study for use as a decorative hanging in the home.

63. Geometric *by Van Dommelen*
Pasted casement cloth, stitchery in yarn and thin thread, and ink on paper make up this geometric approach to a collage wall hanging.

92

64. Grape Vine *by Van Dommelen*
Using fabric on paper is one way the artist can sketch with fabrics.

93

65. Totem Pole *by Van Dommelen*
   Yarn has been applied to this hanging along with newspaper, making it more collage than
wall hanging, if one must classify results.

66. Paper And Stitchery *by Van Dommelen*
A combination of paper and stitches makes up this simple hanging.

67. Root Landscape *by Van Dommelen*

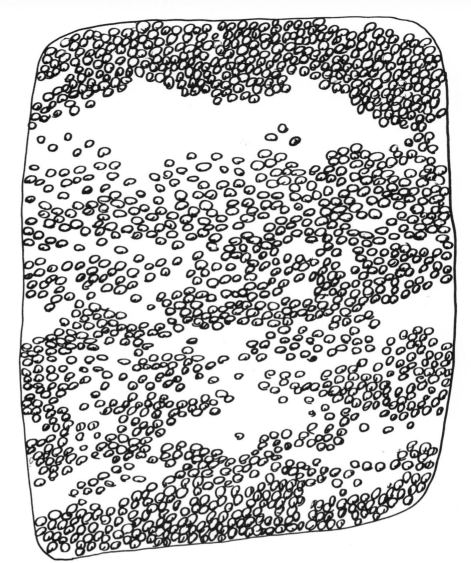

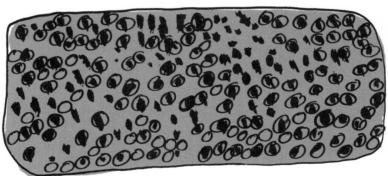

6   hooked wall decorations

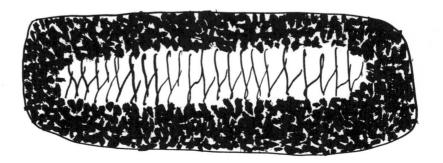

68. Flower Garden *by Veda Reed*
This hooked rug is a painting in wool, nylon, and cotton, and was part of the Designer-Craftsmen U.S.A. 1960 exhibition held at the Museum of Contemporary Crafts. This piece is done in pure rug-hooking technique.

American Craftsmen's Council

6 hooked wall decorations

Today the rug seems to have taken its place on the vertical surfaces of our homes. It has become more painting than rug, and many people have found that the rug is as valid on the wall as it is on the floor. This, of course, is an area for argument, for there are those craftsmen in the field who prefer to see their end product lying flat on a horizontal plane and used for its intended purpose. Regardless of one's philosophy on this subject, it should be mentioned that hooking can and is being utilized as a wall-hanging medium.

Hooking rugs has been a popular method of embellishing the home with hand-crafted objects since the early history of our country. Not only women practiced this art; many men also indulged in the experience of pulling loops through a background material. In earlier times, rags and other stripped fabrics were often used, rather than the prepared woolen and cotton yarns that are employed today, and hooking served many more purposes than it now does. Comforters, lap robes, and other personal and household objects were products of hooking, though rugs seem always to have been the most popular exercise in this medium.

Undoubtedly, it is the Scandinavian *rya* rug, and its new role in contemporary design, which has helped to stimulate an active revival in the art of hooking in this country. Although we never completely ceased working with the hooking medium, our major artists were not as concerned with it and as interested in it as they have been in recent years.

The artist can use the hooking method by itself, or break away from the traditional aspects of hooking and combine it with other techniques. When using hooking for rugs, the craftsman must take into consideration the durability of his product, for it will be subjected to a great deal of hard wear. When applying this same technique to a wall hanging, he is more free to select his background from unusual fabrics. In the hooking of a rug, the craftsman will usually carry out the execution of his design on burlap, which is good, or a heavy grade monk's cloth (duraback), which is far superior to burlap. In the less traditional approaches, one can assume that the fabric will be satisfactory if the hook will pierce the fabric without difficulty.

The process of hooking is simple but rather time-consuming, as is any craft in which manual workmanship is necessary. There are several different needles or machines that can be employed in this craft; their use will depend on the individual and his approach to his immediate problem. A simple crochet hook can be used, or one of the de luxe hooking implements which make loops of pre-set lengths automatically and need only to be guided. Most craftsmen today, however, prefer the crochet hook or punch needle, for these two methods seem to bring them a little closer to the materials with which they are involved. In any case, the result of any equipment is a number of small loops that are pulled or pushed through the background fabric at desired lengths and depths of pile. In working with the crochet hook, the craftsman works from the front of the background fabric and pulls the loops toward him; with the automatic hooker or the punch hooker, the artist works from the reverse side of the fabric and pushes the loops away from him. Any tool you purchase will have explicit instructions, including illustrations, on how to use that particular tool correctly.

In hooking a rug, the designer or craftsman will cover the background completely, as Veda Reed did in "Flower Garden" (fig. 68). Here the entire fabric is covered with small loops which have probably been pulled through with a crochet hook. The design itself is a delightful glimpse into a garden full of flower shapes. Some of the shapes overlap their neighbors, and others seem less dependent on the immediate next-door forms, but all together they give the impression of a natural unweeded garden full of growth and aroma. There is a nice combination of dark and light values in this rug.

The piece of unfinished hooking in Fig. 69 is comprised of hand-stripped heavy wool which has also been pulled and looped by the crochet hook through burlap. Figs. 68 and 69 are quite different from the pieces executed by Jay and Bill Hinz, which are definitely hangings. In Figs. 70 and 71, the viewer gets a real three-dimensional effect from the contrast of hooking against the background. The shapes are fun, and, especially in Fig. 71, there seems to be a rhythmic movement taking place in the shapes; they seem to move across the fabric. In both of these compositions, the craftsmen have approached the level of painting.

Stitchery can also be included with the hooking process. "Study In Red" (fig. 72) is a sample of stitchery and hooking methods on an osnaburg background. The loops have been placed in an open fashion, which gives the appearance of French knots. In "Wheat Field" (fig. 74), the major portion is hooking, closely placed and with deep pile. The chain stitch and the cretan stitch are the main stitches that have been utilized in this hooked hanging on a dark-gray burlap background.

Methods of hooking are good sources for creative work in just about any teaching situation except the early elementary levels. Because of the long, tedious task involved, little children often lose interest after only a short period of time devoted to the piece. It might be possible to incorporate hooking into wall hangings and mural projects, so long as the size of the hooked areas can be kept small and manageable. It is a medium that is highly acceptable for older children in junior and senior high schools. Both the art teacher and the home economics teacher would be well rewarded if they were to consider including this technique in their classroom-project lists. Students at the university level find it an extremely exciting craft and one that is suited to evening "bull sessions." It seems to be a contagious craft, often spreading to those who have

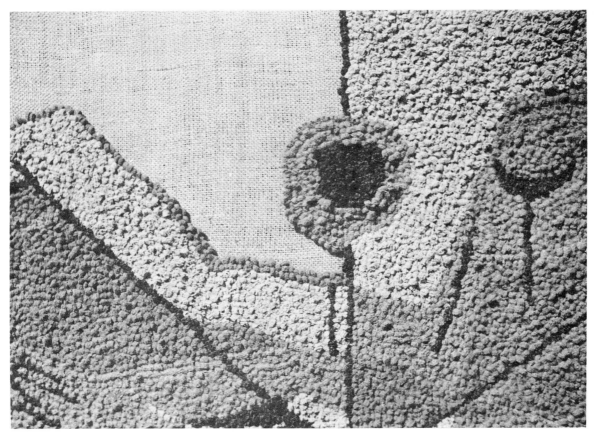

69. Landscape, detail, *by Van Dommelen*
A detail of hooking shows the individual loops that make up the pile in this "in process" piece.

had the opportunity to observe it in action. The author has seen a whole fraternity become involved in hooking because one of their group was working on a rug.

The fact that materials can be obtained easily and at low cost is another reason why many people become interested in and find hooking enjoyable; it also contributes to the adaptability of hooking to use by children in schools. This is not to say that all methods of hooking are inexpensive, because many yarns of high quality are of equally high price. However, the craftsman can strip old blankets, suits, and dresses into narrow pieces for hooking and complete a small or large rug at a minimum of cost. Rug yarns from dime stores can also be used for an inexpensive piece. There are several varieties of cotton and rayon yarns that are low in price and afford the craftsman a small selection of colors. This type of yarn is very good for a beginner, but as you become more advanced you will want to try yarns of higher quality. And, though a frame is essential in the process of hooking, this imposes no great financial burden either. The background fabric that is to be hooked must be stretched across a frame to enable the hooking tool to punch through the fabric effectively. The frame can be made of old lumber; but even with new lumber, a frame costs little more than two to three dollars, and can be reused many times. The frame is usually made with four one- by two-inch strips of pine with mitered corners. It should be of firm construction, because the fabric is stretched on it with considerable tension. The fabric is usually tacked to the edges of the frame, with a two- or three-inch margin left around the entire piece for turning under after the artist has finished the hooking, thus giving the piece its final touches. In Chapter Ten you will see several other ways of presenting the final product as a wall hanging. Unfortunately, as is true for any craft, stores abound in hooking kits and sets that require only that one follow the few directions enclosed with the makings of the product which is to be executed. Most of us feel much more accomplished and proud of our work, however, when the design is our own. It is surprising what we are capable of creating. The late Grandma Moses started her work when she was in her seventies, and became one of the most sought-after artists. Her work, although primitive and childlike, reflected the world as she saw it, not as someone else saw it for her. This is the attitude that should prevail in the execution of rugs and wall hangings, as well as in painting.

70. Hooking by Jay and Bill Hinz

104

A composition of hooking in very basic shapes and interesting varied piles of loops. The background remains unhooked as a part of the composition.

Courtesy of Jay and Bill Hinz

71. Hooking *by Jay and Bill Hinz*
Hooked hangings can be used in any part of the home, as would paintings, to embellish the walls or décor.

Courtesy of Jay and Bill Hinz

105

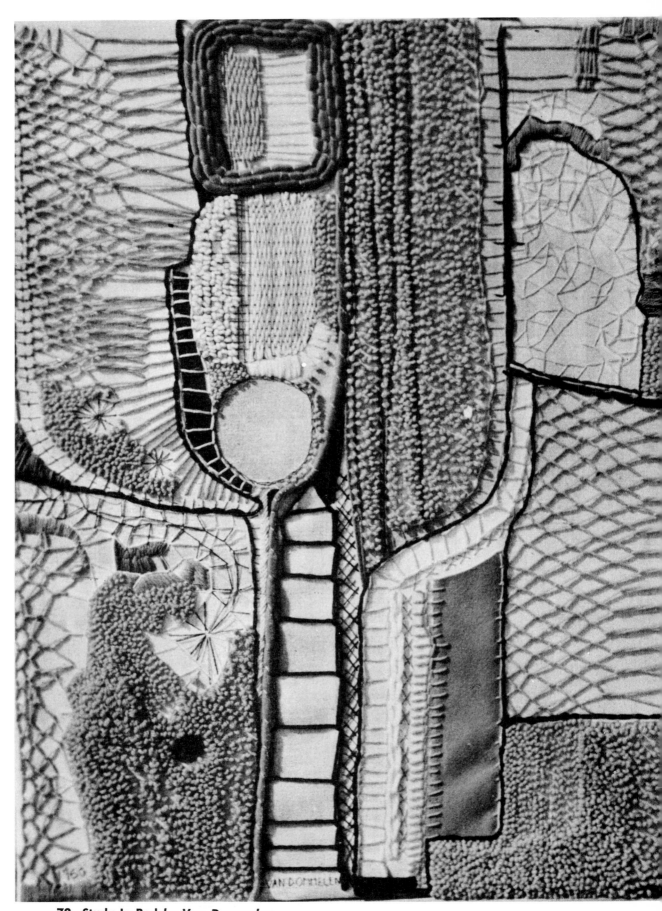

72. Study In Red by Van Dommelen
Unfortunately the color is gone, but the rich texture of this combined-technique hanging still manifests itself. Hooking, stitchery, and appliqué are all part of this composition.

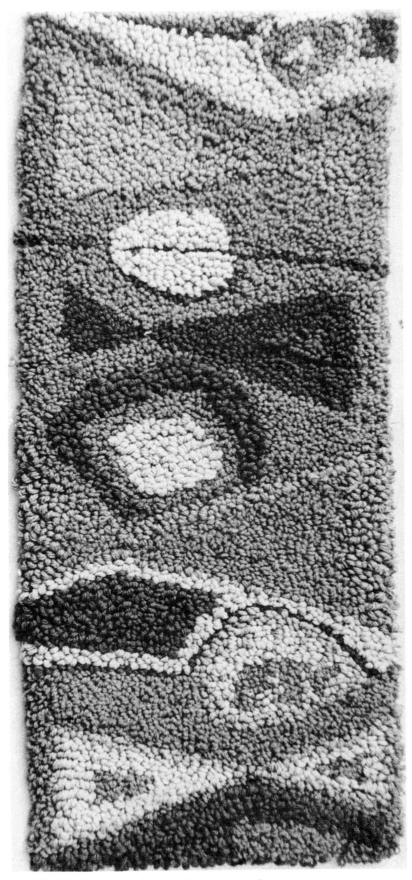

73. Hooked Hanging *by Van Dommelen*

74. Wheat Field *by Van Dommelen*
A combination of stitchery and hooking makes a rich textural hanging.

Collection of Mr. and Mrs. T. DeRocco

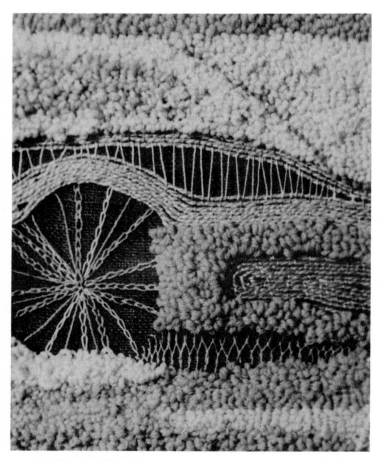

75. Wheat Field, detail

76. Hooked Hanging, detail

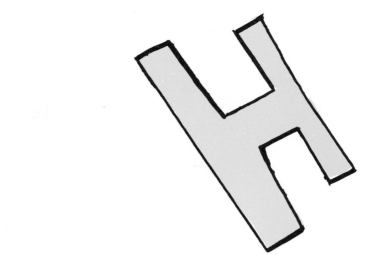

7   **stenciling**

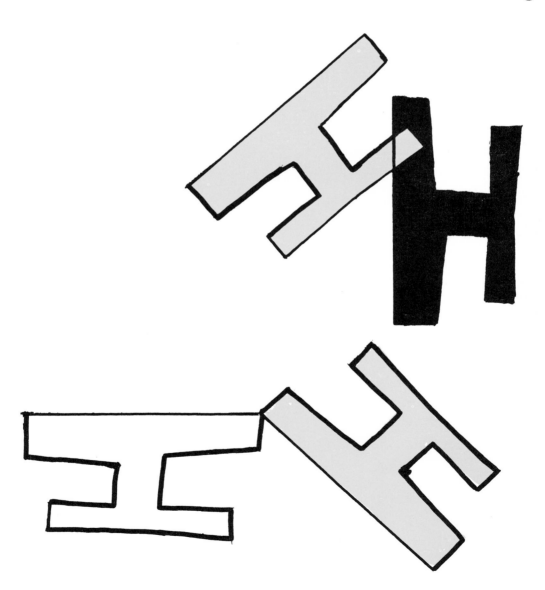

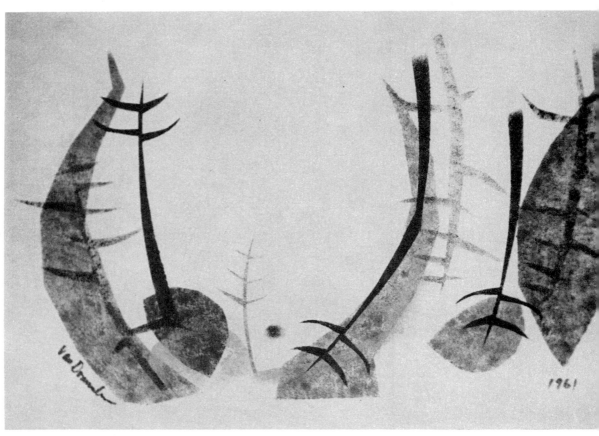

77. Fall Metamorphosis *by Van Dommelen*
Simple tree shapes are repeated several times with slight variations to add interest to the hanging. The background is Belgium linen.

7   stenciling

Stenciling is an art form which reputedly has flourished since Egypt's ancient days. There are also claims that the Chinese and the Romans were adept in this field, as well as the Japanese. Some of its methods are simple and some are very complex; some need few materials and others require many tools to accomplish a successful design.

Most of us are familiar with the quaint designs of early America, and with the stencils used by the French and Germans to add decorative elements to furniture and accessories. The French Provincial *tole* metalwork and the Peter Hunt designs of the United States have long been incorporated into our interior decoration. All of us also know the trite and stereotyped stencil designs that are sold in ten-cent stores across the nation.

Unfortunately, few of us use the great possibilities that stenciling affords the average person as a creative activity. Even more unfortunately, there are many thousands of Americans who depend on the stencils available in retail commercial stores. One of the biggest misuses of the stencil takes place at holiday seasons, when these gaudy, brash, and repulsive designs are dabbed on window panes both in the home and in educational institutions. It is sad to see teachers in our elementary schools promoting uncreative activities, when our main objective should be to teach our children the creative use of their minds and imaginations. It is demoralizing to see commercial stencils depended on to such a large extent at times that should be devoted to creative and expressive work. Delightfully colorful stencils were created in past years, but we should leave these productions to their own age, and prepare to execute more original contributions today.

At this point, we might mention silk-screen printing, which will not be covered in this text although it is a method of printing on textiles that can be used very successfully by the artist and the craftsman. In a sense, it is a stenciling technique, but one that is much more complex than the type we will discuss in this chapter. In the silk-screen process, the craftsman or artist uses a frame which has silk stretched over it very tightly. A stencil is then attached to the underside, and the ink is forced through the exposed silk with a squeegee. However, most artists use the silk-screen method in another, more complicated manner, using glues and tusche as the stencil-forming materials.

The process of making a stencil is very easy, and results in fascinating designs. These, in combination with some of the other methods of wall-hanging production that have been discussed, can make wall-hanging execution more rewarding and meaningful. With stitchery incorporated in a design, the craftsman can achieve interesting textural patterns against the flat qualities of stenciling. However, stenciling need not appear two-dimensional; by overlapping shapes and colors, the craftsman can build intricate spatial structures which have depth and transparency.

The mechanics of stenciling are simple. Using a good, heavy paper, cardboard, or prepared stencil paper from a retail store, the design is traced on the surface and then cut out with a pair of scissors or a razor blade. To prevent the textile paint from deteriorating the stencil too rapidly, wax can be applied to the surface of the paper or board stencil. The prepared retail stencil paper is already waxed for this purpose. The stencil is laid on the surface of the fabric to be printed, then pinned to keep it in position. Color is applied by a stippling action with a stencil brush. Textile paint is used, and the instructions must be followed for successful results. The cutout design is filled in as desired. The shape may be completely filled in, with no fabric showing through the textile paint, or left partially without color. Colors can also be blended within a given shape from one hue to another. When a completely different color is needed, a new shape can be cut out of another piece of cardboard or stenciling paper. However, one design can be repeated many times until the effect desired has been obtained, as in the hanging of "Construction 205" in Fig. 79. Here the letter "H" has been repeated several times, and then enriched with the linear patterns of the felt pen. The felt pen greatly increases the versatility of stenciling.

"Fall Metamorphosis" (fig. 77), "Rocks, Forest and Trees" (fig. 80), and "Lollipop Garden" (fig. 78) are simple compositions using only the stenciling method. Each contains a shape that has been used or repeated several times, some with slight variations, such as Lollipop Garden's tree forms which are changed a little in the center. All three have been printed on Belgium linen, which receives textile paint very nicely, and all have a little stippling effect in some of their shapes.

78. Lollipop Garden *by Van Dommelen*
Lollipop trees and abstract shapes are used sparingly in a childlike style to complete this hanging on linen. This hanging is used in a child's room.

"Canaveral" (fig. 81), which has had stitchery superimposed on the surface, presents a subject which is timely for our generation. In this wall hanging, rockets and spaceships are poised for flight into space. The stitchery adds the linear elements which seem to surround a rocket before it is fired into space, and the stenciling provides heavier shapes to contrast with the lightness of stitchery. The stitchery also adds a textural quality and richness to the composition which would be quite hard to obtain through stenciling alone.

One problem with a stenciling technique of the kind that has been mentioned here is the stylized, clean-cut shape that is often produced. This effect can. be broken through repeated overlapping of shapes and forms, or by the use of stitchery. This is a problem similar to that which was faced in the chapter on press-on tape. In that chapter we solved part of the problem with stitchery techniques. One could also use pasted fabrics to add texture or a three-dimensional quality to a stenciled hanging.

The use of textile paint need not be limited to stenciling processes. By eliminating the stencil and using only the other materials the stenciler employs, a craftsman can approach. his fabric in a "fine art" manner. By using a painter's brush, he can utilize fabric as a canvas and apply the textile paint in bold strokes, thus achieving a free and spontaneous design (fig. 83). This is not to imply that the stenciling technique is still being used, but only that some of the same materials can be investigated in other ways. Blending of the color can be accomplished in the same manner in which the painter blends his oils. This mixing can be done either before application or directly on the fabric canvas. Approaching a painting technique this way means that the artist can eliminate sizing of the canvas through the use of unusual textiles that have many varieties of textures. Almost any fabric could be used for this type of painting, from upholstery fabrics to sheer, transparent marquisettes. The artist could then apply the pure stenciling techniques over the surface of his painting, or he could add stitchery. Marilyn Pappas, whom we read about in Chapter Two on Appliqué, often adds painting strokes to her compositions. Usually they are secondary and not very noticeable; an example of this subordination of painted areas is "Study in Red" (fig. 72), which has had the background of osnaburg painted with textile or stenciling paint by the brush method.

Stenciling is a wonderful medium for any age. Even children in the

117

age group of four to eight years can produce exciting designs. However, with younger children more supervision is necessary in order to help the child see successful results and to prevent him from becoming frustrated in his attempts. The elementary-school child would enjoy a meaningful experience if this medium were introduced as a means of creative expression in the classroom. Certainly it is an unlimited field for homemakers who wish to add decorative elements to their homes. Stenciling and textile painting have an infinite vocabulary with which the housewife could experiment for many uses. Wall hangings are not the only things to be achieved by this technique. Clothing, draperies, pillows, and other household objects could be decorated by the same method.

To "fix" the textile design after you have completed your work, simply iron the fabric with a warm iron. For more permanent fixing, use a little white vinegar in a damp cloth between the stenciled piece and the warm iron. This will enable the piece to be washed often without losing any of the brilliancy of its color.

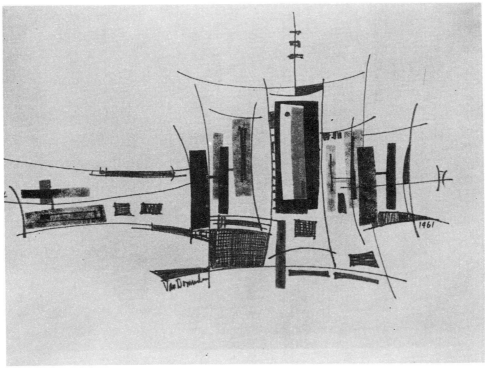

79. Construction 205 by Van Dommelen
   The letter "H" has been used in several positions and in several values to act as the base of this composition.

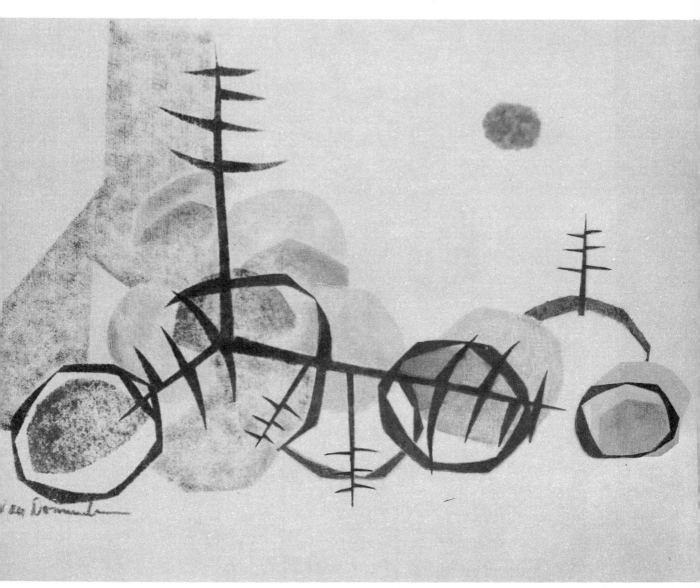

80. Rocks, Forest, And Trees *by Van Dommelen*
Belgium linen has been used as the background for this wall hanging.

81. Canaveral *by Van Dommelen*
Stenciling and stitchery make nice combinations on a wall hanging. Through stitchery the craftsman can bring in a three-dimensional quality.

82. Canaveral, detail, *by Van Dommelen*

121

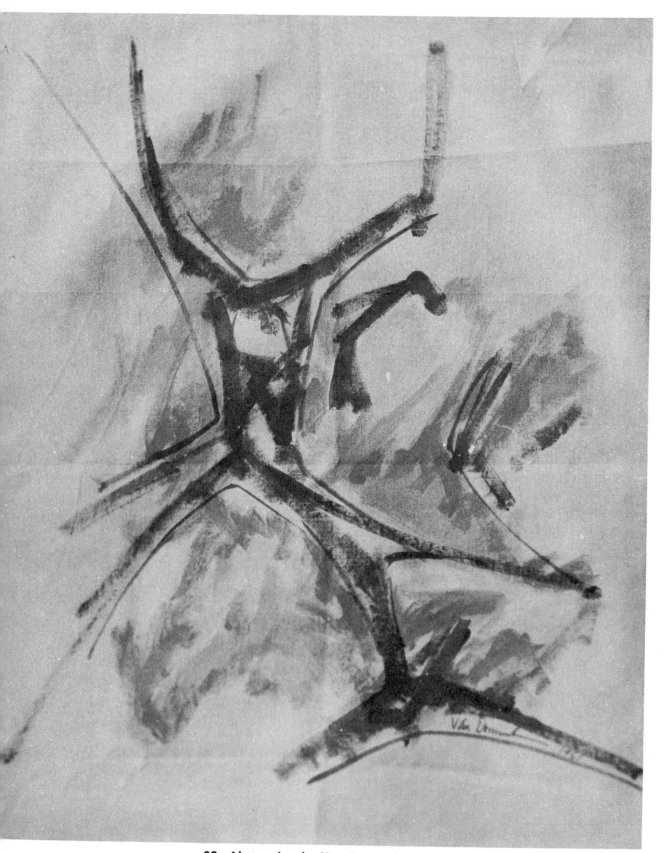

83. Abstraction *by Van Dommelen*
Abstract expressionist painting can be done with stenciling paint instead of oil.

84. Leaf *by Van Dommelen*

8   dyeing

85. Mosaic by Van Dommelen
Crayon batik is a simple project for children. The results can be colorful and fun.

8   dyeing

Many dyeing processes are complicated and involved, requiring a great understanding of dye sources, mordants to fix the dyes, and other chemical properties with which most of us are unfamiliar. But because it is hoped that many laymen will want to incorporate dyeing methods into their work, some elementary methods will be presented in this book. In many cases the artist or craftsman might want to add only a small dyed portion to his hanging, and this should not necessitate his learning all the complex areas of dyeing.

The history of dyed fabrics is a long one which has produced many interesting results for the textile designer. Archeologists have discovered that many primitive groups developed highly technical dyes of a quality that has withstood the test of time. Both the Egyptians and Phoenicians were well known for some of the dyes they produced. The Phoenicians are known especially for the famous Tyrian purple. India has been responsible for many unique methods of decorating fabrics with dyeing procedures. In the time of Nero's reign, Indian textiles influenced the fashion and fabrics of Rome. "The quality of Indian dyeing, too, was proverbial in the Roman world, as we know from a reference in St. Jerome's fourth-century Latin translation of the Bible, Job being made to say that wisdom is even more enduring than the 'dyed colors of India.' " (*Textiles and Ornaments of India*, p. 26.)

Dyes, although very advanced in other countries and societies around the world, were little understood in the United States until after the First World War. Before that time, the Germans monopolized almost the entire field of artificial dyes. Since then, the United States has developed many good dyes. Using these American artificial dyes, the craftsman can produce sparkling colors in wall-hanging design.

One technique of dyeing, and one of the least complicated available to the designer, uses no dye at all. It is highly recommended for upper elementary grades, or wherever students have the skill to use an electric iron. This method is called crayon dyeing, or crayon batik. Drawing techniques are especially successful in crayon batik. A minimum of materials is needed, and this is one reason why designing with a method such as this one can be so highly recommended.

For this process, any background fabric may be used, but a thin, lightweight fabric will do the best job. The design is drawn on the fabric with crayon, first lightly, then with the desired heavy lines and filled-in areas. The design can be "fixed" on the fabric as each step is completed, or the complete composition can be finished before the last process is carried out. In any event, the artist can always return to the drawing step whenever he needs to do so. After the design has been drawn on the fabric, the fabric is pressed between several layers of newspaper with a hot iron. The newspaper will absorb the melted wax and leave only the coloring in the fabric. It is sometimes necessary to repeat the ironing step until all the wax has been removed.

The designing possibilities of the crayon-batik technique are unlimited. "Mosaic" (fig. 85) was drawn in little squares of color on lawn fabric, to achieve a sparkling mosaic quality. The crayon marks are noticeable in some of the areas, but in others the heaviness of the crayon gives a more filled-in appearance. In "Construction 416" (fig. 86), the crayon lines resemble some of the lines we have seen done with felt pen. Many unusual effects can be obtained with this method. "Construction 416" seems to have greater depth than "Mosaic," which has a comparatively flat quality.

"True" batik is a well-known medium, and it is very different from crayon batik. It is certainly a more difficult process, but one that is rewarding and artistically satisfying. Batik is especially characteristic of textile work done in many countries in the Far East. Javanese

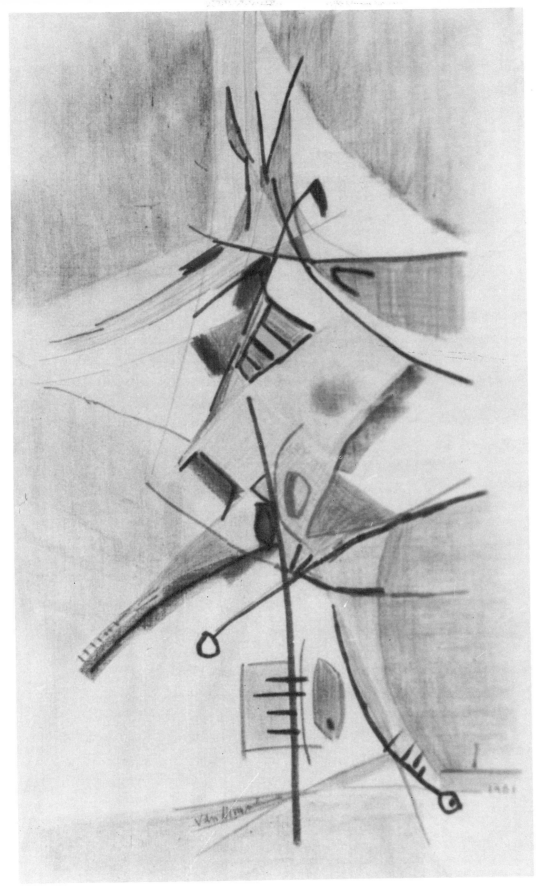

86. Construction 416 by Van Dommelen
Lines, shapes, and space can be accomplished in a design on fabric through dyeing with crayon batik.

batik, however, seems to be the method most often seen and worked with. The patterns and designs of the Javanese batik method are colorful and gay, using rich blue, brown, and cream colors. Regional variations and patterns are designed with symbols and traditional markings in each community doing this wax-resist work. The work from Java and the surrounding islands is intricate and detailed, and when batik was introduced in the United States in the early 1900's, the technique was modified somewhat.

In batik work, after the fabric, which is usually a thin one, has been stretched on a frame, melted wax is brushed onto the fabric into the desired design. The wax is made of beeswax and paraffin, and should be kept at a temperature suitable for brush application. The wax is first painted onto those parts which are to remain white, or the color of the original fabric. The fabric is then dyed; after drying, the second brushing of wax will cover those areas the artist wishes to retain at the first dyeing color. This process is repeated until the design is finished. Although most artists use a sketch for this type of work, quite often they depart from it as they move along in their design. The wax is removed in the same manner as was described in the crayon-batik technique. If excess wax still remains in the fabric, this can be removed with a cleaning fluid.

The batik technique is used by Joseph Almyda (fig. 87) with great proficiency. His shapes and forms are nicely balanced with linear networks and there is a well-balanced understanding of values from dark to light. His work sparkles with rich color.

In all dyeing-with-wax techniques, the dye should never be hotter than the melting point of the wax. Most of the dyes used in this country today are artificial dyes, and are available in ten-cent stores and grocery stores. These are the dyes which are used by housewives for dyeing various household items. The directions which come with the dye are very easy to follow. Of course, the craftsman who wishes to make his own dyes from natural materials can do so. There are many good sources available in libraries covering many different ways to make dyes. Ulla Tollerz used natural hues in the yarns for her hanging (fig. 12); very frequently the Scandinavian craftsman is found using naturally dyed yarns and fabrics.

Many procedures are available for the craftsman to follow, but it is also fun to experiment with dyeing. In Fig. 88, several unorthodox things were done to achieve the final design. A second dyeing

130

131

87. Court Portrait *by Joseph Almyda*
A rich sense of shape and line has been achieved through this composition done in true batik technique.

American Craftsmen's Council

88. Dyed Abstraction *by Van Dommelen*
Dyeing can be creative and enjoyable. This composition was an experimental piece using artificial dyes.

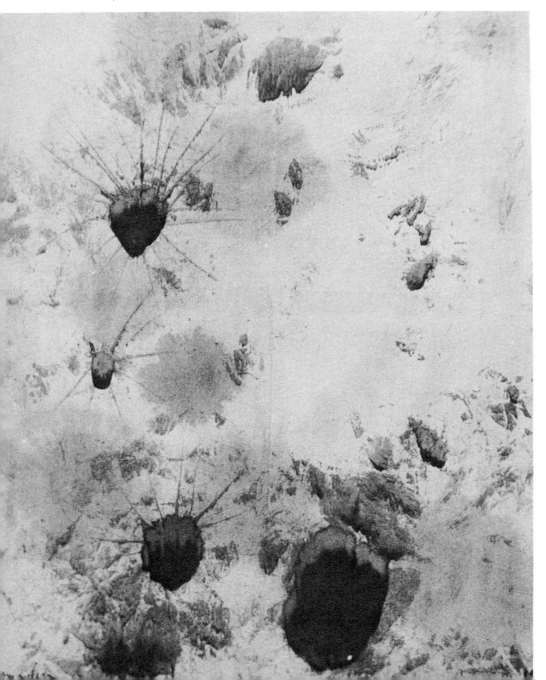

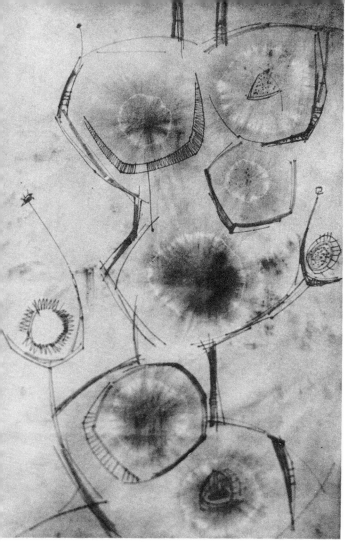

89. Tie-dyeing and Felt Pen *by Van Dommelen*
Many techniques can be combined with dyeing. In this case
the felt pen was used to add linear drawing to the hanging.

immediately followed the first dyeing, before the first was allowed
to dry. This of course caused bleeding of shapes and colors. Also,
several large spots of heavy black dye were put on the fabric, which
was then folded and wrinkled in the hands. The whole composition
was hung to dry, allowing some of the dye to run down the fabric.

Tie-dyeing is another form of dyeing which has become very
popular in the last few years. This is an old art that was highly
developed in India. It is still being practiced there by contemporary
village groups carrying out the old and traditional methods.

133

In this method of dyeing, a portion of the fabric is picked up with the fingertips, and a string or waxed thread is wound very tightly around the point thus formed. The tying is repeated at even or uneven intervals, as desired, on each point thus gathered up. Where the waxed thread has been wound around the fabric, the fabric will remain white, and the exposed parts of the fabric will take on the color of the dye. The cloth should be evenly distributed in the knot if a round clear circle effect is desired in the pattern or form being made. In Fig. 90, Katherine Mangum has carefully tied her fabric to give repeated circular effects. Her tie-dyed fabric is a good example of the complex results which can be accomplished with tie-dyeing. After all the tying is completed, the fabric is submerged in the dye, which should be in a container that will allow plenty of room for the fabric to be completely covered by the dye. This is also true of any other type of dyeing—the whole fabric should be dipped under the dye level at one time, unless the craftsman has a specific reason for not doing this.

After being dyed by any of these processes, the fabric should be rinsed and treated with a mordant; if an artificial dye was used, a mordant is not necessary. The piece is then allowed to dry, and after being pressed with an iron, it is finished, unless some unique way of hanging the work is contemplated.

Tie-dyeing and felt pen were combined in Fig. 89. The fabric was dyed in ordinary artificial dyes from the ten-cent store, and the felt-pen lines were added after the piece had been allowed to dry. Felt-pen lines can be applied when the fabric is wet, different effects being obtained.

Many other techniques can be combined with dyeing, very easily and with fascinating results. Stitchery can be superimposed on dyed areas, or a craftsman might wish to add dyeing to a piece of stitchery. If a piece of stitchery seems to be unsuccessful because of lack of coordination within the design, the piece may be dyed to bring about a more unified color. Stenciling might also be added to dyed fabrics for various effects. And of course the person needing more interesting colors in yarns and threads can take care of the problem by the use of dyes. Ropes and heavy cords, which usually come in a limited number of colors, can be had in greater selection through dyeing to suit the particular needs of the individual craftsman.

134

90. Tie-dyed Fabric by Katherine Mangum
A sample of pure tie-dyeing resulting in characteristics that are truly associated with the craft of tie-dyeing.

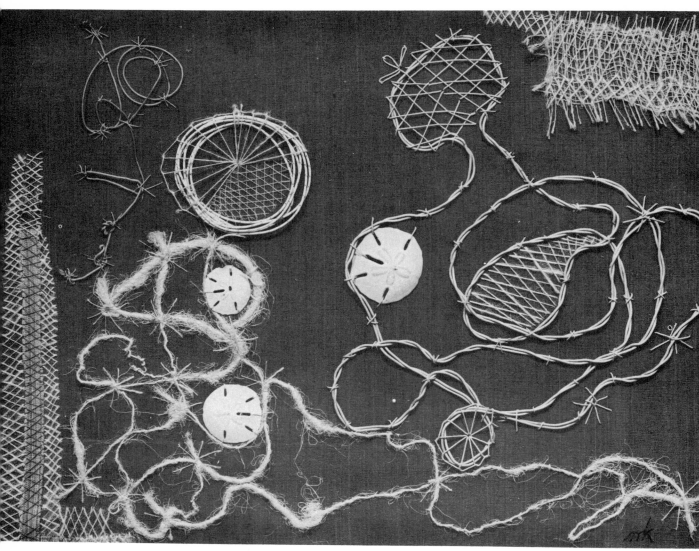

91. Sand Dollars *by Mariska Karasz*

Mariska Karasz often used materials that seem unrelated to wall hangings, but actually were carefully integrated as part of the artistic statement.

Courtesy of Bertha Schaefer Gallery

9   three-dimensional materials

We are slowly discovering that there are few materials that the artist and craftsman cannot use in creating an artistic expression. He has experimented with virtually every material available, and has let little hinder him in his exploration of a world that is continually producing new things for him to assimilate into creative production. We need only look at Mariska Karasz' "Sand Dollars" (fig. 91) wall hanging, which she completed in 1952, to see how three-dimensional materials and objects can be incorporated on fabric to make a decorative hanging. Miss Karasz' philosophy seems to be more than that "whatever can go through a needle can be attached on a hanging," because she also uses objects that can be sewn *through* —in this case, the delicate sand dollar.

The use of three-dimensional objects again raises the question of where the line exists between the creative activities that take place in our society today. There are many hangings that are more sculpture than hangings, and some paintings that are certainly crossing the threshold into the world of stitchery. We saw this with Jean (Hans) Arp's painting, "Dancer" (fig. 61); and if we examine the "painting" by Manolo Millares (fig. 92), which was exhibited at the Guggenheim Museum in the summer of 1960, we immediately ask the question: "Is it a painting, a wall hanging, or a sculpture?" And we have a right to examine this kind of activity in the arts, as well as the subject matter which is being presented. We must at the same time agree that the artist has stimulated our minds with a presentation of form and texture which is unique to our visual experience. Of course, not all wall hangings dealing in three-dimensional materials go to the extremes that we see in the piece in Fig. 92. In a detail of "Textural No. 1" (fig. 93), a plastic scouring pad has been utilized for parts of the composition, and the cardtacks which had been used to hold the work while it was in process were left in the work to create an addition of metallic sparkle. In "Textural No. 1," the surface is relatively flat as compared to Fig. 92. But even so, the three-dimensional objects, especially the scouring pad, introduce unique visual experiences through the varied surface heights of the materials.

Many types of metals can be incorporated into a wall hanging, especially if they are flat or not too heavy. Obviously, if an attached piece is too heavy, the fabric will not hang properly.

Marie Fedon, a student interested in textures and in experimentation with materials, used a copper screen as a part of her stitchery in Fig. 94. The stitches penetrate the screen in order to hold the metal to the linen background. The whole composition, which, by the way, is the first attempt by Mrs. Fedon, is an interesting statement of architectural forms—rich, formal, and determined in design execution.

Some of the most experimental work in the use of three-dimensional materials is taking place among the weavers. We will not make a detailed study of the process of the art of weaving, but it would certainly be a mistake not to mention the important hangings that are being created by the loom artists.

One of these exploring weavers is Luella Williams, of Ithaca, New York. Her imaginative approach has led her into fields and forests to pick weeds and seeds to enrich her weaving experiences. Her work naturally produces a hanging rich with the colors of nature, and echoes the meadows and fields from which she draws her materials. She weaves broomcorn, columbine, and lemon lily leaves, to name a few, into the warp threads of the loom. In Fig. 95, the nubbly and prickly weeds can be seen in the warp threads, making a pattern of stripes and oval shapes that are irregular and soft.

Another craftsman who uses grasses and twigs in her work is Mary Buskirk. Her work in plant growth as elements in design is not as extreme as Miss Williams'. Mrs. Buskirk actually does more experimentation and exploration in yarns and threads than in the use of three-dimensional objects. However, in Fig. 96 an osier branch has been added, which sweeps across the hanging as in

92. Painting 61 _by Manolo Millares_
This painting illustrates the closeness of collage, wall-hanging methods, and painting.
Courtesy the Solomon R. Guggenheim Museum

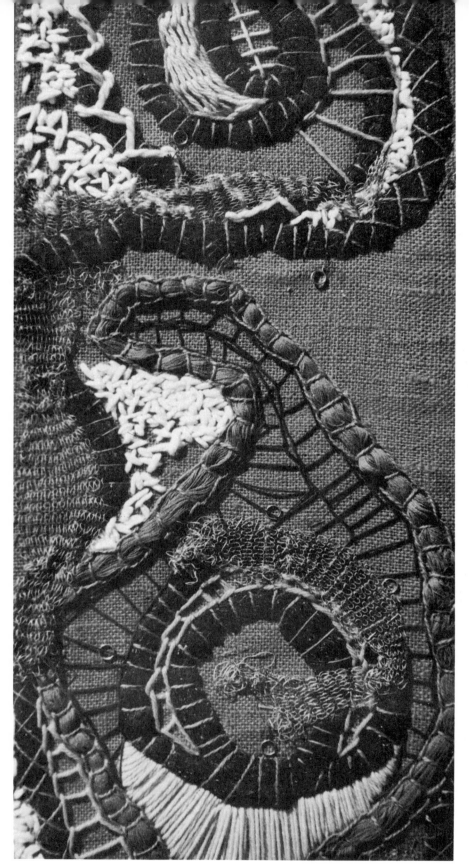

93. Textural No. 1, detail, *by Van Dommelen*
A detailed view of this wall hanging shows the variety of materials that one can use in wall-hanging design.

a spring breeze. Her work is delicate and feminine, with transparent qualities that are a little like those achieved by Mrs. Tollerz.

Alice Parrott's work reflects the desert by which she is surrounded and in which she works. Mrs. Parrott, although not an American Indian, has captured the feeling of the art of the tribes in the Southwest. The wall hanging in Fig. 97, open in design, creates an atmosphere of space woven into the composition. Along with its traditional God's-eyes and lilac sticks, this hanging contributes to the new and contemporary approaches the craftsman is using today to express his philosophies and ideas. Most of our good craftsmen working in their respective areas depend heavily on the techniques of the past and the stimulation of the past.

This is true not only of Mrs. Parrott's approach to weaving, but also of the way in which Alice Adams works. She has a deep understanding, through extended studies of the processes, of the Aubusson tapestries and the way in which they are made. Her study in France led her to the tapestry or wall hanging in Fig. 98, which is a completely contemporary composition using old tapestry techniques. The work actually becomes three-dimensional as twists of yarn pop out from the surface of the fabric and disappear back into the warp threads from where they came. This three-dimensional hanging gives the impression of an essay with paint rather than of a craft execution.

"The craftsman generally stands apart from the activities of the 'fine artists,' yet he is closely associated with the 'fine' arts. Again and again, we see the strong influence of and likeness to painting and sculpture in his work. Throughout the crafts, the craftsman is attempting to break away from the limitations of traditional forms and the conventional functions of the objects he creates. However, this does not mean that he has neglected utilitarian values completely, but rather, that he is exploring new concepts of contemporary design.

"For many years the crafts have played a minor role in the arts, but recently a strong movement toward closing this gap in importance and significance has become evident." (Design At Work: Its Forms And Functions, p.27)

As this gap closes, the craftsman reaches more and more into the realm of the fine artist. His work manifests the same discipline that is characteristic of the painter, the sculptor, and the print-maker.

As the fine artist explores new means of expressing his creative philosophies, so does the craftsman; and as the craftsman delves into the world of the artist, he finds new materials that are adaptable to his media. At times we question his use of these materials and the manner in which he uses them. The fact that we question his approach to his work does not imply that he has no right to make the kind of statements that he is presenting to the art world, but only that we as thinking beings must question all events that take place in our lives. In the case of decorative wall hangings, the individual designer and the individual viewer must each take a stand on what he considers the areas in which creative craftsmen may work and successfully bring about meaningful experiences. The wall-hanging specialist must decide where a line is to be drawn between his work as a craftsman and that work produced by the fine artist. To what length is he permitted to go before he definitely enters another area of concentration, and if he does enter this field, can this be considered acceptable behavior?

We have seen briefly some of the materials that the artist-craftsman has incorporated into his work in the area of wall-hanging design. The designer in textiles is not the only artist who is beginning to bring new uses of materials into focus for esthetic enjoyment. The Museum of Modern Art illustrated to us in its "The Art Of Assemblage" exhibition that the sculptor has entered very controversial materials into his works in using metals and foreign objects. These objects are pieces of "junk" he accumulates from back alleys and trash collectors, only to bring to the public a different interpretation of these forms. Obviously, the layman is going to find fault with his goals and aims, just as the spectator will question those unfamiliar objects found in the composition of a textile wall hanging.

Louise Nevelson's wall panel (fig. 99) illustrates another way in which a craftsman or a sculptor solves the problem of creating for wall decoration. This panel illustrates the area of materials into which the artist is moving with force and determination. Crates, cut boards, and slats, usually painted a flat, dull color, are all the ingredients of this composition; yet the viewer's eye jumps with delight across the openings as it discovers the shape hidden in each compartment. Miss Nevelson's work has taken the art world by storm. Her work can be seen in the Museum of Modern Art in New York and in major museums across the country.

144

94. Stitchery with Screen *by Marie Fedon*
Metal screen adds to the rich texture of stitches in this architectural type hanging.

Courtesy of the artist

95. Weaving with Weeds *by Luella Williams*
Weeds and grasses are only a part of nature which can be incorporated into warm, ear**[**
compositions.

*American Craftsmen's Cour***[**

This is not a wall hanging—at least this work has never been given that name—but if it were suspended from a wall surface by wire it might be. If this leaves the reader with a question unanswered, that is the purpose. Let each person make his own decision. At this time, sculpture, painting, and the crafts have become closely meshed, and it is difficult for anyone to make an honest, accurate appraisal of the identity of many art objects.

It is the craftsman's responsibility to present the work he is doing with all the integrity he can muster, and to accompany this integrity with standards that he accumulates through his years of investigation and study in the area he has chosen for his artistic expression. His work should honestly reflect his own philosophies and ideas; this in itself will guide his work toward a more meaningful statement, one worthy of thought for the layman and the understanding fellow craftsman.

His contribution of new materials will be thoughtfully presented, rather than used merely for effect. The use of new materials does not in itself qualify the end product as a great work of art; for with these newly introduced materials there must be an honest reason for their use in the composition.

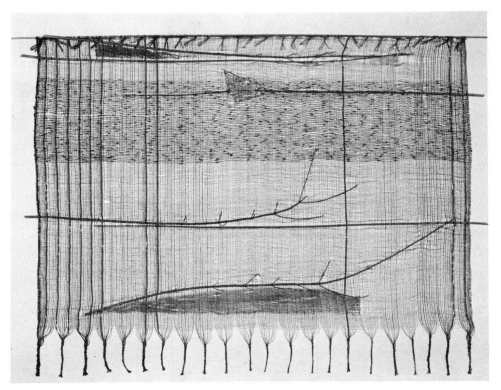

96. Hangng With Osier Branches *by Mary Buskirk*
Twigs and branches can be used as three-dimensional materials in wall hangings, whether they are woven or stitched into the fabric.

American Craftsmen's Council

97. God's-eye Hanging *by Alice Parrott*
Mrs. Parrott uses lilac sticks as the basis for a God's-eye, which is a symbol of protection for the Huichol Indians.

American Craftsmen's Council

148

98. Wall Hanging *by Alice Adams*
In this weaving by Adams, the heavy knotted groups of yarns emerge like materials in a three-dimensional bas-relief sculpture.

99. Wall Panel *by Louise Nevelson*
A wall sculpture of wooden boxes and cut wooden shapes is another form of wall decoration which can be constructed in the home.

New York University Art Collection

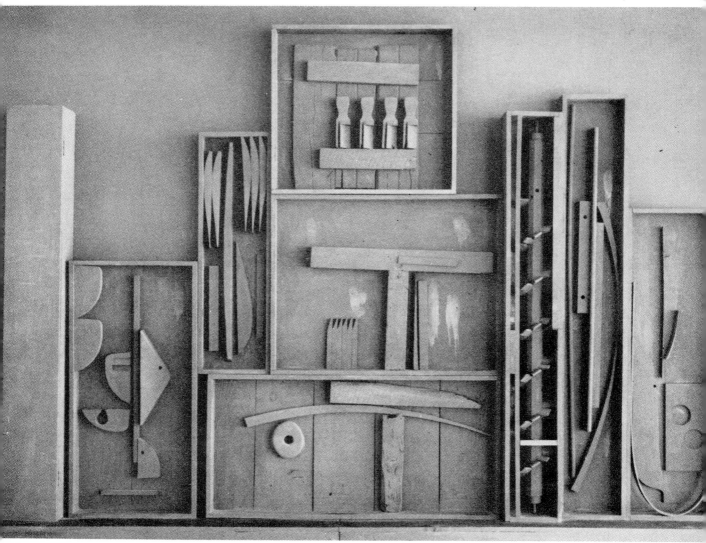

10   **mounting and hanging**

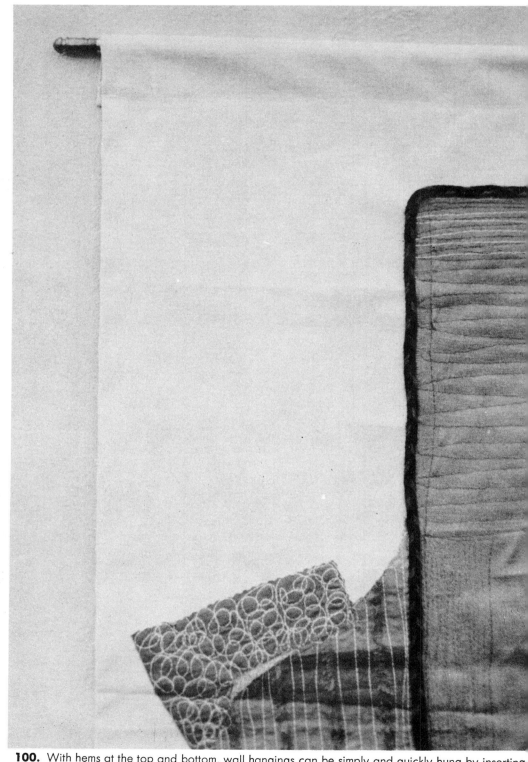

154

100. With hems at the top and bottom, wall hangings can be simply and quickly hung by inserting a dowel or rod through the hem.

10   mounting and hanging

Finishing the completed wall hanging is an important and integral part of the design you have created. No work looks well if the craftsmanship is sloppy and incomplete. Jean Ray Laury once wrote to me concerning an exhibition, "I was disappointed by the lack of craftsmanship in most of the work." The hangings of three craftsmen ". . . were the only ones that were 'finished' and properly hung [made provisions for hanging]." (Letter to Van Dommelen, Jan. 20, 1961)

There are ways in which to mount your wall hanging, and "you are the only one who can decide what setting your handiwork deserves when you are finished with it. Its future must be dictated by its intended purpose and surroundings. Will it travel or will it stay in the same place indefinitely? What other demands will be put upon it?" (*Adventures In Stitches*, p. 122).

Too many craftsmen are concerned only with the creative experiments they are conducting, and give little thought to how this end work will appear in the final stage. Even a poor design can be improved by proper mounting or hanging. But, more imortant, it must be remembered that one can ruin a good composition simply by not giving adequate attention to the finished hanging.

One of the greatest mistakes that the beginner makes is that he does not allow for enough material to surround the piece for the important step of mounting. In starting a piece, leave a wide border around the design; this will mean that you can do any type of finishing when you are ready. It will also mean that you will not need to add extra fabric around the piece, or possibly worry about the edge fraying because of lack of border fabric.

Here are several approaches to completing your piece for hanging:

1. If the wall hanging has been worked on a fabric that has a selvage, all that is necessary is to create hems at top and bottom. After this has been done, a wooden dowel can be inserted into the hem at the top and allowed to project slightly from either side. Another dowel can be put into the bottom hem to weight the piece so that it will hang better. This one need not project outside the hem if you do not want the weighting device to show (fig. 100).

2. The second method of working with fabric that has a selvage is to use strips of wood of a size that will not overpower the piece, yet will act as a hanging device at the top and a weight at the bottom. Walnut, cherry, redwood can be used, or even a piece of pine. Do not use a varnish finish, but simply rub with an oil finish. The hanging can be attached to the strips by tacking, using very small tacks (fig. 101).

3. The stretching method is a very popular way of preparing your hangings. This method is especially good for fabrics that have puckered and will not hang nicely. One approach is to staple the hanging to Homosote or some other type of wallboard, carefully pulling your fabric and stapling each of the four sides alternately until the piece has been firmly attached to the board. The staples and the turned-under edges can then be taped to give a more finished appearance to the rear view (fig. 102).

4. Another way to stretch a hanging is to lace the piece to the board (fig. 103). This is more time-consuming, but very effective. The craftsman needs only to draw the raw edges around to the back of the board and lace back and forth, first the two side edges, then the top and bottom, until the piece is firmly in place. Remember to check the grain of the fabric to make sure it is straight on the front. If the fabric grain is not running straight on the front surface, the lacing job will look sloppy.

There are many other ways to stretch and hang your piece. The method you choose should be determined by the function you wish to express in the piece. Many artists stretch the background as one would a canvas for painting, and then work directly on its surface.

101. A wooden strip attached at the top and the bottom make for an interesting method of hanging your work. The wooden strips can also be sewn on with an attractive couching stitch.

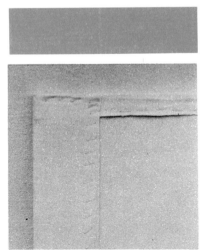

102. A fast and adequate method of stretching is shown here with the use of stapling. The staples can then be covered with tape.

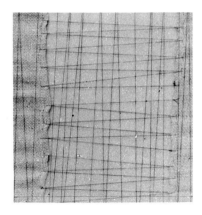

103. More time-consuming than stapling, but very effective, is the lacing method of stretching.

157

Remember that you must decide the finishing touches. Also remember that this is as important as the design you have created.

When a piece has been stretched it is usually because the artist is planning to frame the hanging rather than hang it like a tapestry. Choose your frame carefully. Keep it simple and plain and it will play an integral part in the hanging rather than detract from it.

Once the piece is completed, take care to place it in its proper setting in the home. If you feel that the piece is a success, you might send it to an exhibition. It is a thrilling experience to see your piece accepted in a highly rated show. Craft magazines always list the approaching competitive shows.

One of the advantages of using a non-stretching method is that the hanging is easier to send to exhibitions. If this is not of major concern to you, then choose the method which will satisfy you best. Try all the ways and you will have a better understanding of each and its problems. However, if you intend to send exhibits across the country, you will find that a hanging that can be readily rolled in a compact package is far less expensive to send than one that is framed and must be crated for shipping.

The artist-craftsman enjoys seeing one or several of his hangings in a permanent setting in one of the country's leading museums, but there are many other uses that are just as important to a craftsman who designs objects of beauty and value. One of the greatest thrills a designer or craftsman can experience is to walk into the home of an acquaintance and see one of his hangings displayed as an integrated part of the home. This is proof that the work is appreciated and wanted—that it has taken the eye and gained the appreciation of a person interested in fine things.

The home has many wonderful places in which to display colorful and decorative wall hangings. In fact, there are so many places and uses for them that it is impossible to mention them all in a short chapter.

One point that should be stressed is the importance of using care in exhibiting a hanging in the home. It is certainly necessary that the craftsman execute the piece with the utmost workmanship, so that when it has finally been placed in its setting, it will be a beautiful addition to the room. It should not be hurriedly and sloppily put on just any wall. Instead, its placement should be considered in relation to the objects, colors, and furniture surrounding it.

104. A headboard is a colorful means of exhibiting your appliqué in a bedroom. This one is by Jean Ray Laury.

Courtesy of House Beautiful

Evaluate the place where it will hang. Will the hanging balance nicely with the objects around it? A hanging seems more suited to asymmetrical than to symmetrical balance. Will it pick up other lines in the room and not give the wall a choppy and cut-up appearance? Will the viewer be able to look at it without difficulty?

Don't be afraid to use unusual places for hanging the piece you have created or purchased. A headboard makes a unique contribution to the décor of a bedroom. The one created by Jean Ray Laury adds just the touch that complements the other materials and textures in the room. The design, inspired by "Dandelions," gives a soft quality to the bed and the furnishings around it (fig. 104).

A corner in a room that could possibly be dead space makes a charming place to display crafts. A wall hanging completes a collection of pottery, enameling, and wood pieces in Fig. 105. Setting up such an area is an inexpensive way to bring beauty into a living room.

Another place that is always suitable for a wall hanging is a hallway. A wall hanging above a small chest makes for an inviting spot; a visitor is immediately drawn to exciting color and an atmosphere of individuality (fig. 106).

Above all, wall hangings are meant to be seen. They are like paintings, and demand important situations within the home. Because few people have incorporated them into their homes as yet, they are unusual, and this is added reason for the individual with a sense of curiosity to have one in his home.

105. A dead corner in an apartment is an interesting display spot for crafts. A wall hanging enhances the whole arrangement. Photo by Mike Lynch.

106. Jean Ray Laury's wall hanging of an apple makes a colorful addition to a dull hallway.
Courtesy of House Beautiful

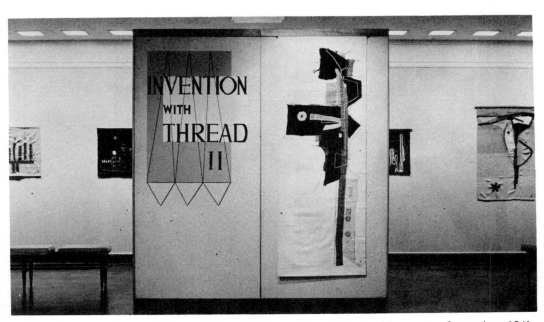

107. The "Invention with Thread II" exhibition at Montclair Art Museum in September 1961 illustrates the magnificence of hangings in the setting of a museum. Photo by Jean Lange.
Courtesy of Montclair Art Museum, Montclair, New Jersey

108. Yarns, threads, and cords from the dime stores or yarn shops, or saved from odds and ends, should be accumulated for stitchery, appliqué, and machine work. The bigger the variety you have, the more interesting the wall hanging becomes.

The choice of materials for constructing wall hangings is unlimited. You as an artist will be limited only by your ingenuity and imagination. There are materials available to the craftsman that are not in yarn departments or fabric shops; these you will discover as your ideas develop, and as you begin to accumulate quantities of things you may one day use on the hangings you are creating. There are many inexpensive materials to begin with, and there are also many very expensive ones. The choice is, of course, entirely up to the individual, with his personal budget. It is not necessary to become involved in great expense in designing your wall hangings. There are many sources of supply at your fingertips. To get a good backlog of fabrics and yarns, start making inquiries of relatives and friends. You will be amazed at the quantity of yarns and fabrics they may have stored away in boxes and drawers. After you have exhausted these sources, watch for sales in small fabric shops. One can find very interesting materials to employ in the creation of hangings. Besides remnants, samples of upholstery fabrics are very good for background material. Also scout about your district for mill-end stores where you can buy beautiful linens, woolens, and other novelty woven textiles for next to nothing in price. All this probably sounds self-evident, but many people are not good scroungers, and can use this information.

The designer should consider the durability of his material. Will it hold up through sunlight, washing, and cleaning? How frequently washing or dry-cleaning may be necessary will depend not only on whether the hanging is light or dark in color, but on where it is to be placed. A good gauge of the frequency of cleaning necessary should be found in your curtains and draperies, which pick up the dust, soot, tobacco smoke, or other soiling elements in a room's atmosphere.

Is the piece to hang naturally, or will it be stretched and framed?

Does the background material go well with the yarns and fabrics to be applied to the surface? They should complement or contrast —whichever result is wanted by the craftsman. There are no laws which must be followed.

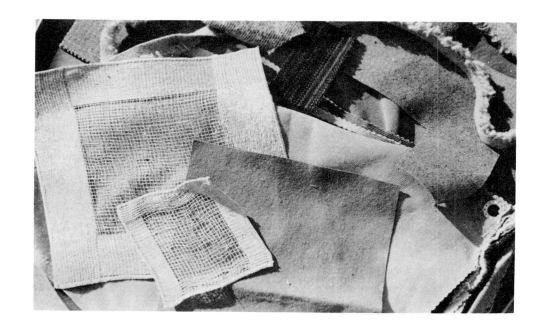

Fabrics

There are many fabrics which can be used in different ways for hangings. Here are a few suggestions for you to investigate and experiment with.

1. *Burlap.* This is a good background material which is ideal for beginners. It is available in many colors, and is very inexpensive. One can do much experimenting without running up a large account. The difficulty with burlap, however, is the fact that it is not a durable material. It fades easily, and after a few years will begin to show rot areas. If it has been stretched to a great degree, the fibers will slowly disintegrate. Another disadvantage of burlap is its open-weave quality. Often wall colors or backing-board colors will show through the fabric when it is hung or stretched.

2. *Cotton.* Jean Ray Laury uses cotton very successfully for hand appliqué; it is also good for machine appliqué. It has a tendency to pucker when heavy yarns are used for stitchery on its surface, but lightweight flosses can be nicely stitched to it. If the piece is to be washed and ironed often, cotton is a durable and lasting fabric to use. It is usually sunfast and pre-shrunk. It is found in a wide price range and is easily available. Some good cottons to use are percale, pima, and polished cotton.

3. *Drill or duck.* Both are heavy textiles and inexpensive ones. They are excellent for use with a machine. Because of their heavy quality and strength, they will not pucker when used with a sewing machine. However, they are not easy to use with stitchery. It is difficult to pull threads of any large size through the weave; the craftsman soon has sore fingers. Color selection is limited—few establishments have anything but white and natural—but if the artist is ambitious he can dye it many colors. It is also good for use with paste, fabrics, and felt pen.

4. *Felt.* Although felt is somewhat expensive for the beginner, there are many wonderful colors available. One problem with felt is its tendency to work out of shape in some situations. This is especially true when it is used with the sewing machine. But it does afford a nice soft background, and, if necessary, one can finish the edges without difficulty.

5. *Handwoven fabrics.* These fabrics are beautiful and are found in hundreds of wonderful textures. They are expensive, but are excellent for stitchery. Mariska Karasz often used handwoven fabrics.

6. *Linen.* This is by far the best textile to use for wall hangings. Aside from its quality of permanence, it can be obtained in many colors that are fun and exciting. Also, it is easy to use in stitchery, appliqué, and with the sewing machine. The only problem with linen is that it is often too expensive. The beginner would be wise to save linen as a more advanced material for backgrounds.

7. *Marquisette.* Both nylon and dacron marquisette are available today. This transparent fabric provides the craftsman with a chance to create interesting hangings that are seen from both sides when used as room dividers. Stitchery is interesting on this fabric, but is sometimes difficult to do because the back, as well as the front, is seen. This means that one's craftsmanship must be at its best.

8. *Organdy.* An excellent fabric to superimpose on colorful cottons. Because of its semitransparent characteristics, the craftsman can obtain nice variations in color by using it in this way. It works well with sewing-machine appliqué, is not expensive, and is available in all parts of the country.

9. *Wool.* Wool is an excellent textile to use as a background material. In addition to being obtainable in an infinitely wide range of colors, it offers unlimited possibilities to the craftsman in the number of weaves available. The only problem is that of moths when the hanging is being stored; finding that your prize hanging has been attacked would be most disconcerting.

General Materials

Here is a sample list of materials that can be accumulated for use in the designing of wall hangings. Not everyone would want to use all of these things, but it might be a good idea to have a few unusual pieces of material around for that moment when you see how some of them can be incorporated into your work.

1. Hairnets
2. Cords, ropes, and strings (used for tying boxes)
3. Remnants and upholstery samples
4. Pieces of crocheted and knitted material
5. Sewing notions, such as rickrack
6. Old clothes (coats, dresses, pants, and sweaters)
7. Weeds, shells, and possibly small rocks (natural materials)
8. Pieces of interesting paper and foil
9. Plastic scouring pads, copper screening, and plastic screening

10. Shoelaces and old purses with bead and other decorations
11. Cobbler's lace and automobile trimmings
12. Beads and plastic rings
13. Small pieces of wood and small twigs
14. Cork and tiles
15. Small plastic and rubber tubing

BOARDS

Of the boards that are available on the market today for stretching wall hangings, Homosote and Masonite are probably the best. Masonite is hard, and very good for use with the lacing techniques. It is durable and well-built. It is a dark-brown material that comes in several weights. The size of the piece to be stretched will determine what weight board you will want. Homosote is a fibrous board, and is used with the stapling method of stretching the hanging. It is thicker, but not as heavy as Masonite. Both these boards are available at a building supply depot or lumber yard. Other wallboards can be used with good results.

SKETCHBOOK

A sketchbook is good for keeping records of your designs and of the wall hangings you have completed. Little notes giving background information on various facets of wall-hanging design might also be included. The author keeps a constant sketchbook covering all aspects of his creative work. Clippings and pictures are often used as illustrative material, along with the drawing and writing put in the book for personal use. This notebook or sketchbook is a personal diary, and is not intended for general reading. It is fun to watch the number of your sketchbooks accumulate on the shelf as your ideas multiply through the years.

Suggested Materials By Chapters

Because there are many varied materials and pieces of equipment needed for the many approaches to wall-hanging design presented in this book, here is a chapter-by-chapter list of items needed. This will enable the beginner to collect his tools in an orderly fashion as he begins to experiment with the different techniques.

1. Stitchery

1. Needles of various sizes. Tapestry No. 20 and wool darners 5/0-1/0 are most suitable, but a good variety of other sizes should be kept on hand.
2. Background materials
   a. Burlap
   b. Linen
   c. Osnaburg
   d. Drill or duck
   e. See the section on fabrics in this chapter.
3. Scissors
4. Yarns, threads, floss, and other small rope
5. Optional materials
   a. Stretcher or frame
   b. Embroidery hoop
   c. Other materials to be embroidered onto background fabric, such as beads, wool, plastic rings, etc.

2. Appliqué

1. Needles
2. Background fabrics suitable for the type of appliqué you are planning
3. Scissors
4. Threads of many colors for machine and hand appliqué
5. Sewing machine, if machine appliqué is planned

3. Paste, Fabric, and Felt Pen

1. Elmer's Glue-All or a good substitute
2. Background fabrics. (See the section on fabrics in this chapter.)
3. Small pieces of textured and colored fabrics collected from different sources
4. Felt pens—one or more colors
5. A board on which to stretch the piece of background fabric
6. Scissors

4. Press-on tape and Felt Pen

1. Press-on tape of different colors
2. Press-on mending patches
3. Background fabric (the fabric should be smooth for good contact with the press-on tape)
4. Felt pens—one or more colors. These are rather expensive, so collect them slowly for less strain on the budget.
5. Safe electric iron and ironing board. If little children are to use the ironing board, make sure it can be lowered to a functional height for them.
6. Threads and other materials that might be combined with press-on tape

5. Paper, Collage, and Fabrics

1. Papers of different kinds
   a. Newspaper (possibly in other languages for more interesting effects)
   b. Construction paper of different colors
2. Fabrics and fabric swatches

3. Threads and yarns
4. Drawing ink and felt pens
5. Elmer's Glue-All and scissors

6. Hooked Wall Decorations
1. Frame for hooking
2. Background fabric
3. Hooking tool
4. Yarn or stripped fabric for hooking
5. Yarns and threads for stitchery, if stitchery is to be combined with hooking
6. Tacks for attaching fabric to frame
7. Hammer
8. Stripping machine for stripping fabric (optional)

7. Stenciling
1. Stencil brush
2. Stencil paint or textile paint
3. Stencil paper or heavy cardboard
4. Background fabric
5. Pins
6. Stitchery materials, if stitchery is to be combined with stenciling
7. Turpentine to clean brushes
8. Newspapers to protect working surface

8. Dyeing
1. Crayon batik
   a. Crayons
   b. Lightweight background fabric (lawn)
   c. Newspapers
   d. Electric iron and ironing board
2. Batik
   a. Lightweight fabric (often silk)
   b. Frame
   c. Beeswax ($2/3$) and paraffin ($1/3$)
   d. Japanese brushes
   e. Container for wax
   f. Dyes
   g. Container for dyeing
   h. Stove or burner for melting wax
3. Tie-dyeing
   a. String or waxed thread
   b. Dye
   c. Fabric
   d. Dye container
   e. Other materials as necessary, if combination of techniques is contemplated

9. Three-Dimensional Materials
1. Background fabric or material
2. The materials to be attached and the manner in which they are attached will depend on your problem and the results you are seeking. This is a chapter where the imagination must take over completely.

SUPPLIERS OF MATERIALS

At times the teacher needs large quantities of materials which are unavailable in the community in which she teaches. This list of suppliers and companies is for her, and for persons working in isolated areas where supplies are unobtainable. In many cases, these companies give discount prices for large orders; this is especially adaptable to teaching situations. This is not an extended list, but it gives the beginner a place to start gathering materials.

Fabrics

1. Utrecht Linens, Inc.
   119 West 57th Street
   New York 19, N. Y.

   Dealer in excellent Belgium linens for the craftsman. This fabric is inexpensive, of various textures, but available only in white and natural.

2. Bon Bazar, Ltd.
   149 Waverly Place
   New York 14, N. Y.

   A large selection of decorator burlaps in a beautiful range of colors. Inexpensive, and good for the beginner.

3. Bloomfield Woolen Co.
   Bloomfield, Indiana

   Very beautiful woolen fabric of heavy quality. This can be obtained in large pieces for wall hangings, or stripped in narrow widths for hooking wall hangings and rugs.

Yarns

1. J. C. Yarn Company
   111 Spring Street
   New York 12, N. Y.

   One can buy yarns by the pound here and get a package with a great variety of texture and color.

2. Lily Mills Company
   Handweaving Department
   Shelby, North Carolina

   Many interesting yarns—both inexpensive and medium-price. Novelty yarns and hand-weaving yarns can contribute much to stitchery.

3. Paternayan Bros., Inc.
   312 East 95th Street
   New York 28, N. Y.

   Wonderful selection of yarns for tapestry, crewel work, rugs, and knitting. The quality is the best in the yarn business. Certainly not expensive for the quality one gets.

Miscellaneous Materials

1. American Crayon Company
   Sandusky, Ohio

   This company carries not only stenciling materials, but materials of all kinds. Write for a catalog for a complete list of supplies.

2. M. Grumbacher, Inc.
   460 West 34th Street
   New York 1, N. Y.

   This company has a huge selection of brushes. Stenciling brushes can be obtained here, as well as Japanese brushes.

3. Rit Products Division
   Indianapolis, Indiana

   Artificial dyes.

4. Singer Sewing Machine Co.
   149 Broadway
   New York 6, N. Y.

   The Singer Company has many booklets and other printed material available through their stores on the operation of machines. Many interesting sewing materials can be obtained through their chain stores.

5. Speedry Products, Inc.
   Richmond Hill 18, N. Y.

   Felt pens of all colors.

6. David Traum Co., Inc.
   15 East 26th Street
   New York 10, N. Y.

   This company deals in press-on tape which is available in many colors and textures.

America Fabrics Magazine
The Textile Arts
A Book of Tapestries

bibliography

Embroidery Design
Your Embroidery
Primitive Art
Craft Horizons

Adventures In Stitches
Creative Stitchery
Dictionary of Embroidery Stitches
Embroidery Book
Textiles & Ornaments of India
Bayeux Tapestry
American Needlework
Creating Hooked Rugs

bibliography

1. Adams, Edward, George Pappas, and David B. Van Dommelen. *Design At Work: Its Forms And Functions*. Pennsylvania State University, University Park, Pa., 1961.
2. *American Fabrics Magazine*. New York: Reporter Publications, Inc.
3. Birrell, Verla. *The Textile Arts*. New York: Harper & Brothers, 1959.
4. Blazkova, J. *A Book of Tapestries*. London: Spring Books, 1957.
5. Booker, Molly. *Embroidery Design*. London and New York: Studio Publications, Inc., 1935.
6. Brooks, Helen. *Your Embroidery*. Peoria, Ill.: Charles A. Bennett Co., 1949.
7. Christensen, Erwin O. *Primitive Art*. New York: Thomas Y. Crowell Co., 1955.
8. Conran, Terence. *Printed Textile Design*. London and New York: Studio Publications, Inc., 1957.
9. *Craft Horizons*. New York: American Craftsmen's Council.
10. "Creative Stitchery Series." *House Beautiful* (October 1961), pp. 204—211.
11. "Creative Stitchery Series." *House Beautiful* (November 1961), pp. 206—208.

12. Dean, Beryl. *Ecclesiastical Embroidery*. London: B. T. Batsford Ltd., 1958.
13. *Design Quarterly*. Walker Art Center, Minneapolis, Minn.
14. Harbeson, Georgiana Brown. *American Needlework*. New York: Coward-McCann, Inc., 1938.
15. Karasz, Mariska. *Adventures In Stitches*. New York: Funk & Wagnalls Company, Inc., revised 1959.
16. Kepes, György. *Language Of Vision*. Chicago: Paul Theobold and Co., 1944.
17. Laury, Jean Ray. "Creative Stitchery." *House Beautiful* (January 1960), pp. 52—55.
18. MacLagan, Eric. *The Bayeux Tapestry*. Middlesex, England: King Penguin Books, revised 1953.
19. Michel, Adelaide. *Stenciling*. Peoria, Ill.: Manual Arts Press, 1920.
20. Moholy-Nagy, Laszlo. *The New Vision*. New York: Wittenborn, Schultz, Inc., 1949.
21. Rorimer, James J. *The Cloisters*. Metropolitan Museum of Art, New York, 1951.
22. Rozaire, Charles E. "Pictographs At Burro Flats." *Ventura County Historical Society Quarterly*, February 1959.
23. Scott, Robert Gillam. *Design Fundamentals*. New York: Mc-Graw-Hill Book Co., 1950.
24. Thesiger, Ernest. *Adventures In Embroidery*. London and New York: Studio Publications, Inc., 1941.
25. Thomas, Mary. *Dictionary of Embroidery Stitches*. New York: William Morrow and Co., 1935.
26. Thomas, Mary. *Embroidery Book*. New York: William Morrow and Co., 1936.
27. Underhill, Vera Bisbee. *Creating Hooked Rugs*. New York: Coward-McCann, Inc., 1952.
28. "Wall Hangings: Part One." *Interiors* (May 1961), Vol. CXX, No. 10, pp. 118—121.
29. "Wall Hangings: Part Two." *Interiors* (June 1961), Vol. CXX, No. 11, pp. 120—125.
30. Weibel, Adele Coulin. *Two Thousand Years of Textiles*. New York: Pantheon Books, Inc., 1952.
31. Wheeler, Monroe. *Textiles and Ornaments of India*. Museum of Modern Art, New York, 1956.

about the author

about the author

David B. Van Dommelen was born in Grand Rapids, Michigan, and entered the art world in 1949. In addition to a bachelor of arts degree in art education and a master of arts degree from Michigan State University, he has a degree from the Francis Harrington School of Professional Interior Decoration of Chicago. His interests are many and varied. He was an elementary art consultant for Warren Consolidated Schools in Michigan and taught at Pennsylvania State University. He is currently teaching design at the University of Maine. His writing includes articles on Eskimo folklore and co-authorship of *Design At Work: Its Forms And Functions*. He has exhibited wall hangings in over twenty exhibitions in the last five years, and has had one-man shows in many museums across the country.

Mr. Van Dommelen has this to say about his work:

"My field of concentration in wall hangings contributes as much to the Fine Arts as does contemporary painting. In fact, my goal *is* painting—in yarns, threads, and fabrics. I find it as valid as painting in oils or water colors. To me, the stitch of yarn or the stitch of the sewing machine has as much message as the stroke of a brush. I find myself in a medium that is completely unexplored, ready to be discovered and opened to the world like a polar island.

"Most of my ideas come from nature, which to me is so much more perfect than man. I usually am inspired by flowers, rocks, or just the beauty in color that our world has to offer the spectator.

"Although I do use the city as a source of ideas, I feel that the city is usually much less inviting than our natural world. This is probably why I am found in the middle of natural beauty—surrounded by the greenery of our world instead of the choking atmosphere of our cities."

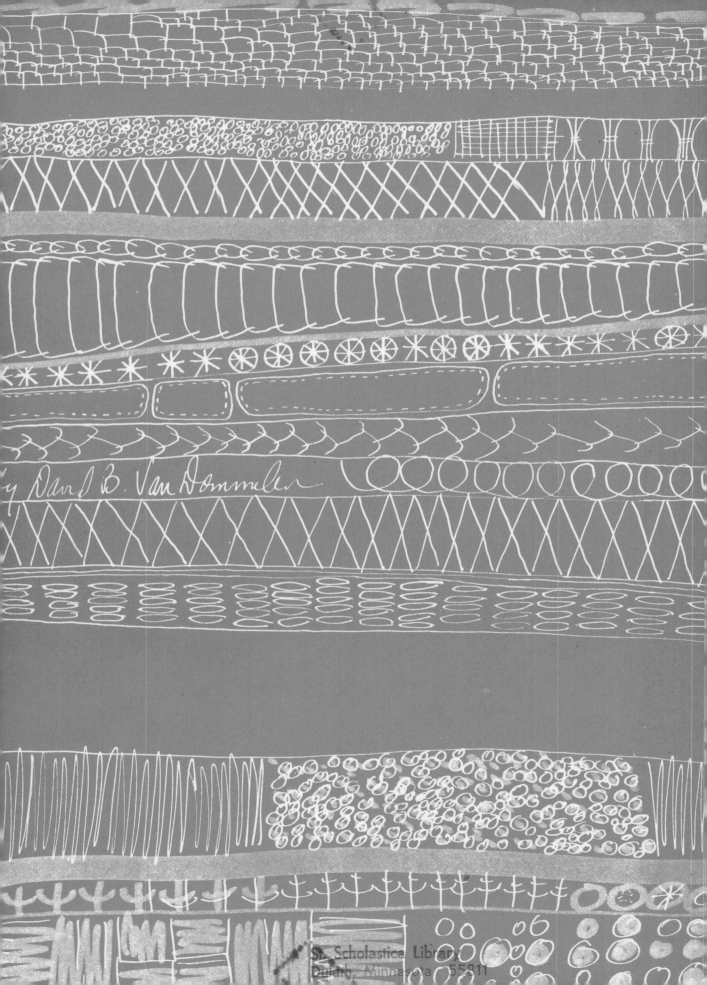